Read On . . . Audiobooks

Recent Titles in Libraries Unlimited Read On Series
Barry Trott, Series Editor

Read On . . . Historical Fiction: Reading Lists for Every Taste
Brad Hooper

Read On . . . Horror Fiction: Reading Lists for Every Taste
June Michele Pulliam and Anthony J. Fonseca

Read On . . . Fantasy Fiction: Reading Lists for Every Taste
Neil Hollands

Read On . . . Crime Fiction: Reading Lists for Every Taste
Barry Trott

Read On . . . Women's Fiction: Reading Lists for Every Taste
Rebecca Vnuk

Read On . . . Life Stories: Reading Lists for Every Taste
Rosalind Reisner

Read On . . . Science Fiction: Reading Lists for Every Taste
Steven A. Torres-Roman

Read On . . . Audiobooks

Reading Lists for Every Taste

Joyce G. Saricks

Read On Series
Barry Trott, Series Editor

 LIBRARIES UNLIMITED

AN IMPRINT OF ABC-CLIO, LLC
Santa Barbara, California • Denver, Colorado • Oxford, England

Library of Congress Cataloging-in-Publication Data

Saricks, Joyce G.
  Read On— Audiobooks : Reading Lists for Every Taste / Joyce G. Saricks.
    p. cm. — (Read On Series)
  Summary: "With more than 300 original annotations in some 60 thematic lists, this one-of-a kind compilation opens the world of audiobooks to listeners and librarians alike"— Provided by publisher.
  Includes bibliographical references and index.
  ISBN 978-1-59158-804-7 (pbk. : acid-free paper) — ISBN 978-1-59158-807-8 (ebook)   1. Audiobooks—United States—Catalogs.   2. Libraries—Special collections—Audiobooks.   3. Readers' advisory services—United States.   I. Title.
  ZA4750.S37   2011
  011'.384—dc22   2010051372

ISBN: 978-1-59158-804-7
EISBN: 978-1-59158-807-8

15   14   13   12   11   1   2   3   4   5

This book is also available on the World Wide Web as an eBook.
Visit www.abc-clio.com for details.

Libraries Unlimited
An Imprint of ABC-CLIO, LLC

ABC-CLIO, LLC
130 Cremona Drive, P.O. Box 1911
Santa Barbara, California 93116-1911

This book is printed on acid-free paper ∞

Manufactured in the United States of America

For Chris, who also loves to listen to stories of every kind

Contents

Series Foreword

Welcome to Libraries Unlimited's Read On series of fiction and nonfiction genre guides for readers' advisors and for readers. The Read On series introduces readers and those who work with them to new ways of looking at books, genres, and reading interests.

Over the past decade, readers' advisory services have become vital in public libraries. A quick glance at the schedule of any library conference at the state or national level will reveal a wealth of programs on various aspects of connecting readers to books they will enjoy. Working with unfamiliar genres or types of reading can be a challenge, particularly for those new to the field. Equally, readers may find it a bit overwhelming to look for books outside their favorite authors and preferred reading interests. The titles in the Read On series offer you a new way to approach reading:

- they introduce you a broad sampling of materials available in a given genre;
- they offer you new directions to explore in a genre—through appeal features and unconventional topics;
- they help readers' advisors better understand and navigate genres with which they are less familiar;
- and they provide reading lists that you can use to create quick displays, include on your library Web sites and in the library newsletter, or to hand out to readers.

The lists in the Read On series are arranged in sections based on appeal characteristics—story, character, setting, and language (as described in Joyce Saricks's *Reader's Advisory Services in the Public Library*, 3d ed., ALA Editions, 2005), with a fifth section on mood. These are hidden elements of a book that attract readers. Remember that a book can have multiple appeal factors; and sometimes readers are drawn to a particular book for several factors, while other times for only one. In the Read On lists, titles are placed according to their primary appeal characteristics, and then put into a list that reflects common reading interests. So if you are working with a reader who loves fantasy that features quests for magical objects or a reader who is interested in memoirs with a strong sense of place you will be able to find a list of titles whose main appeal centers around this search. Each list indicates a title that is an especially good starting place for readers, an exemplar of that appeal characteristic.

Story is perhaps the most basic appeal characteristic. It relates to the plot of the book—what are the elements of the tale? Is the emphasis more on the people or the situations? Is the story action focused or more interior? Is it funny? Scary?

Many readers are drawn to the books they love by the characters. The character appeal reflects such aspects as whether there are lots of characters or only a single main character; are the characters easily recognizable types? Do the characters grow and change over the course of the story? What are the characters' occupations?

Setting covers a range of elements that might appeal to readers. What is the time period or geographic locale of the tale? How much does the author describe the surroundings of the story? Does the reader feel as though he or she is "there," when reading the book? Are there special features such as the monastic location of Ellis Peters's Brother Cadfael mysteries or the small town setting of Jan Karon's Mitford series?

Although not traditionally considered appeal characteristic, mood is important to readers as well. It relates to how the author uses the tools of narrative—language, pacing, story, and character—to create a feeling for the work. Mood can be difficult to quantify because the reader brings his or her own feelings to the story as well. Mood really asks how does the book make the reader feel? Creepy? Refreshed? Joyful? Sad?

Finally, the language appeal brings together titles where the author's writing style draws the reader. This can be anything from a lyrical prose style with lots of flourishes to a spare use of language à la Hemingway. Humor, snappy dialog, word-play, recipes, and other language elements all have the potential to attract readers.

Dig into these lists. Use them to find new titles and authors in a genre that you love, or as a guide to expand your knowledge of a new type of writing. . . . Above all, read, enjoy, and remember—never apologize for your reading tastes!

Barry Trott
Series Editor

Acknowledgments

First, thanks to Barry Trott for suggesting this idea and to him and Barbara Ittner for shepherding me through the process. Their enthusiasm and suggestions have been invaluable, and I am endlessly grateful for their support.

Thanks also to the Downers Grove Public Library and the Department of Literature and Audio Services staff who have been endlessly helpful in providing me with audiobooks from their collection and from surrounding libraries. I am so lucky to live in a community with a great library and in a state with a great library system.

I have relied on friends and colleagues for suggestions throughout, and I thank you all. In particular, I have been lucky in my readers, who, in spite of this ordeal, have remained good friends. Marty Charles slogged through all the annotations and checked bibliographic details. A thankless task, but she has also shared some of my favorite listening experiences on long car trips—and will continue to do so, I hope. Sue O'Brien read and fearlessly critiqued all the annotations. For almost 20 years she has read and edited my writing, and I am grateful for her keen eye, excellent suggestions, and enthusiasm. Neal Wyatt continues to inspire me to explore deeper into the art of readers' advisory. Her thoughtful suggestions and spot-on criticisms have improved this manuscript and kept me on my toes.

My deep and abiding pleasure in stories read aloud—and now in audiobooks—has been aided and abetted by my husband Chris, with whom I have shared this agreeable addiction for more than 40 years. Our listening today may be more diverse than in the first years of our marriage when we read aloud the novels of Wilkie Collins, *The Lord of the Rings*, and *The Divine Comedy*, along with David Dary's excellent *True Tales of the Old Time Plains* and more. Now we share audiobooks, easier on our voices and on my stomach on twisting roads. Thanks always to Chris for reading and commenting on this manuscript and for sharing my pleasure in audiobooks.

Introduction

I have frequently acknowledged my addiction to audiobooks. I love listening, having a story wash over me while driving, shopping, walking, or waiting (in line or for an appointment). Audiobooks consistently see me through times when reading actual books would be inconvenient. The titles described in this book represent but a fraction of the audiobooks I have enjoyed over the past few decades. Frankly, I'm afraid to add up the hours they represent, even though I know that most of my listening was done while I was involved in other activities. Indeed, one of the greatest advantages of audiobooks is that listening is quite conducive to multitasking and thus allows avid readers to fit more stories into their lives. Because so many library patrons feel the same way, it is important for readers' advisors to become familiar with the format and the stars of audiobook narration.

In the past decades, audiobooks have become one of the most popular sections of the library; and today they account for a significant portion of the materials budget. Audiobook circulation grows so much every year that it often seems impossible to keep up with the demands of fans, both in terms of our collections and the kind of assistance we can provide in helping them find the listening experiences they seek. Furthermore, librarians and listeners have become increasingly aware of the dearth of materials available to help them make selections of what to listen to next. The chapters in this book are grouped by conventional appeal terms—language, mood, story, character, and setting. Each chapter offers lists to help listeners match their interests and sensibilities to audiobook suggestions. The lists can be used to identify listen-alikes and "next listens," as well as to post on your library Web site or in the library newsletter, or to create multimedia displays. Because all of the titles in this guide are recommended, this book might also be employed for collection development.

Within the appeal categories, these lists offer a wide range of listening experiences, both enjoyable and provocative. While I hope listeners will find new titles to enjoy, I expect these lists will remind them of their favorite books as well. Because audiobooks are so portable, they often expand a listener's "reading" time. Why not revisit favorite authors and titles through another medium rather than simply rereading? I also hope these lists take listeners in directions they might never have explored before. Why not try an author or a subject you might never sit down and read but are willing to listen to while gardening or walking or driving? These lists can help listeners and librarians alike explore the pleasures of audiobooks.

The Audiobook Phenomenon

So why have audiobooks become so popular? That devices for listening have become more convenient is surely one reason. When I first listened to audiobooks as a child, I had 78 rpm records—and I still have the record player and many recordings. In the 1980s, after years of reading aloud with my husband, I rediscovered audiobooks on tape. They changed my life. Instead of reading to each other on long car trips, we listened, sometimes choosing titles for the whole family. My walkman went with me everywhere, as my MP3 player does today.

Of course, audiobook quality has changed dramatically—literally—since the 1980s. While some older recordings were excellent, others were read in a monotone voice—so as not to detract from the author's words, I was told. Disaster! Classics were almost impossible to listen to, and nonfiction was even worse. Deadly, dry, uninviting. But as the 1990s progressed, all that changed. Publishers began hiring narrators with real acting experience whose skill at drawing readers into stories started a revolution in the industry. All this coincided with a time when commuters faced longer and longer drive times, and our lives became more mobile. Audiobooks provided surefire entertainment in even the worst traffic jam or airport delay.

Convenience aside, I've always believed there's a deeper reason for the popularity of audiobooks: we stop reading aloud, sharing a listening experience, at too young an age. Audiobooks allow us to go back to those carefree days when we always had someone to read us a good story. Like children, we adults are hungry for story. With audiobooks we don't need to set aside time in our busy lives to sit and read. We can listen almost anytime, frequently while we're engaged in an activity that doesn't require our full attention. The story can distract us from the effects of a tedious task such as exercising or weeding the garden. Audiobooks make stories portable. They fit our schedules and enliven our days.

Working with Listeners and Audiobooks

While every listener is different, a few generalizations hold true. Audiobook listeners tend to be adventurous listeners. They are often willing to try books on audio that they wouldn't necessarily take time to read. Fiction readers sometimes see this as an opportunity to explore nonfiction, for example; and listeners can often be lured to move beyond their usual choices by the promise of an interesting title or a popular narrator.

Narrators often play a more important role in listener choices than the author, title, or subject of the audiobook. Many audiobook fans have narrators they love—and will listen to everything they read—as well as narrators they don't like and might avoid listening to at all costs. This makes it both harder and easier to choose titles and to advise listeners. It makes it harder, because in addition to finding a title the listener might like, we must also consider the appeal of the narrator. It makes it easier, because with so many factors involved, we can simply suggest a range of titles and remind listeners to bring back the titles that don't suit them.

There are also issues unique to the audiobook format. If a book is poorly written, every fault is magnified in the audio version. Listeners can't escape the clunky dialog, poor characterizations, or gaping holes in the plot; they hear every word. A good narrator can make a good book better, but even the best narrators can't save poorly written books.

Trigger points (graphic sex, gratuitous violence, and profanity) that potentially offend readers and listeners are amplified by an audio format, especially if we are listening with headphones. There's no escaping a violent beating or vicious language—it's right there in our heads.

Another disadvantage of audiobooks is that the listener doesn't have an opportunity to reflect, unless he stops the recording or goes back to listen again. With traditional book formats it is easier to scan the pages to find what you're looking for. Audio is not the answer for every book or every listening need.

On the other hand, anything with dialect is much more easily understood on audio. Students assigned Zora Neale Hurston's classic novel *Their Eyes Were Watching God* often do better with the audio version. Dialect heard is more readily understood than dialect read in print.

Long, story-centered novels also work well in audio for many listeners. The story can be listened to in one long stretch or in short pieces, but the narrator does all the work. We listeners just sit back and enjoy. I confess I'm often surprised at how quickly some of the really big books move. I become so engrossed in the story and the pleasure of listening that I barely notice how many hours I've spent on the book. I struggled to read Orhan Pamuk's *My Name Is Red*, but when those 400+ pages were translated into 20 hours of listening in John Lee's seductive narration, I was completely caught up in the story and time flew by.

And for those who don't make nonfiction their first reading choice, nonfiction on audio becomes more accessible. Skilled narrators animate the facts and details and create absorbing listening experiences from books that might otherwise seem overwhelming. I personally would never have managed David McCullough's *The Path between the Seas: The Creation of the Panama Canal,*

1870–1914 or *The Great Bridge: The Epic Story of the Building of the Brooklyn Bridge* without the audio versions.

A Note about This Book

Within these pages are annotated lists of audiobook titles I have listened to over the years. This is not a definitive list of the best audiobooks. These titles have given me pleasure or caused me to think; their narrators created listening experiences I'd like to share, ones you may also be interesting in trying. As I compiled the lists, I despaired that no matter how many books I listed, the lists could never be complete. What about all the titles I loved listening to but couldn't fit into any of the lists? And worse, what about those titles I remember fondly as cassettes that have never made the transition to compact disc or downloadable audiobooks? Alas, this book cannot be a complete catalog of the great experiences to be had through audiobooks but is instead a glimpse into the life of a compulsive listener and represents many hours lost in the pleasures of a story well told.

Most of the titles included are fiction, because for years that was the focus of my reading and listening. As nonfiction recordings became more inviting and my work expanded to include that area as well, I listened to more, and a smattering of interesting nonfiction titles appear on some lists. Some 330 titles, the majority of which were recorded after 2000, are described.

The titles included are held at public libraries as compact discs with a very few exceptions. It was with great sadness that I had to eliminate some titles that were only available on cassette. Many of these titles—David von Drehle's excellent *Triangle: The Fire that Changed America* and Marne Davis Kellogg's delightful caper *Brilliance* to name but two—deserve to be re-issued in today's popular formats.

My hope is that this book might assist librarians in understanding the special connections that exist between listeners and audiobooks and can serve as a tool for collection development and readers' (or listeners') advisory. Hard though the concept is to accept for an addicted listener like me, listening to audiobooks is not for everyone. Some listeners find the narrator voice too distracting or become so involved in the story that they cannot do anything but listen. For those for whom driving becomes hazardous when under the influence of an audiobook, I recommend abstinence—at least in the car. Others who may have tried them in the early days of the industry (before the mid-1990s) should be encouraged to try them again. After all, when borrowed from the library, they're free. They can simply be returned if they prove unsatisfactory.

Of course, I hope this wouldn't happen, and that instead a new favorite title or narrator or a new direction to pursue is discovered. This book offers a path to all these possibilities. Among these pages are captivating stories to keep families entertained on car trips, groupings of novels that take you beyond subject headings, fiction and nonfiction that transport you to other times and places, classics waiting to be "resurrected" and rediscovered, and atmospheric tales that are enhanced when read aloud. While the lists address a range of topics and moods, all provide dependable listening experiences. So browse these lists at your leisure, and find something new to enjoy—and, in many cases, hard to forget.

Symbols Used in Annotations

▶   Start Here

♟   Audio Award Winner

♛   Book Award Winner

Ⓨ Ⓐ   YA Friendly

♨   For Book Discussions

Chapter One

Language/Voice

In the context of reading, we think of *language* as writing style, which is more or less important depending on the book. In audio, however, language transcends writing style to incorporate the narrator's voice and is thus always crucial. While lyrical prose can resonate in lovely fashion in audio versions and a chatty, conversational style can enliven a long drive, listeners are at the mercy of the narrator's voice and skill to deliver not just the author's words, but the entire world of story as well. This makes the narrator's voice the prime consideration in an audio book. We need to ask, Does the narrator's voice work for the story? Does it reflect characters accurately and capture the tone set by the author? Does the narrator use precise accents and inflections to place characters geographically or by background? And just how well does the narrator distinguish between genders and among characters? These are questions more at the core of a listening experience than simply the words narrated.

Correct pronunciation is another consideration. Whether they are foreign terms, unusual or unfamiliar English words, or proper names in any language, words must be pronounced correctly or the mistakes create distractions that pull listeners out of the story. Too many errors cause listeners not to trust the narrator's voice.

Cadence, the rhythm of conversation and description, is also vital. Some authors write with a particular cadence, and hearing it on audio brings it to life. Stories that the narrator rushes through or draws out too long will throw the listener off, ruining the experience.

In the end, the most critical factor is for the listener to accept the narrator as the true voice of the book. If not, then the audio will not work; if so, then the delights of language can be experienced—and the world of the story will unfold.

The lists below highlight narrator skills, showcasing some of the best readers in the business—readers who can make characters, places, and stories come alive and who always manage to get the sound, pace, and inflection just right. Some of these suggestions include authors who are adept at narrating their own books. Other titles boast multiple narrators or a full cast. Popular and acclaimed narrators are also featured.

All the World's an Audiobook: Full Cast Readings

Two areas in which fiction and drama overlap are full cast readings of novels and radio versions with music and sound effects. These are not plays per se, but these types of projects allow the ensemble cast to interact as they perform their roles and convey the distinctive mood of the piece.

Brooks, Max

World War Z: An Oral History of the Zombie War. Read by Max Brooks, Alan Alda, Carl Reiner, Jurgen Prochnow, Waleed Zuiater, Dean Edwards, Michelle Kholos, Maz Jobrani, Mark Hamill, Henry Rollins, Eamonn Walker, Ajay Naidu, John Turturro, Rob Reiner, Jay O. Sanders, Dennis Boutsikaris, Becky Ann Baker, Steve Park, Frank Kamai, and John McElroy. 2006. Books on Tape (Abridged). ISBN: 9781415933510. 6 hrs. ♒

Think *War of the Worlds* with zombies. Add a cast of thousands (including Alan Alda, Mark Hamill, and Carl Reiner), "you are there" sound effects, and grisly tales of battles and their aftermath, and you've got a compelling "mockumentary." The deadpan delivery of the first-person accounts adds to the dramatic flavor and earnestness. The audio format makes events and reactions all the more real and adds to our pleasure.

Horror; Humor.

Card, Orson Scott

Ender's Game. **Ender Wiggin Series.** Read by Stefan Rudnicki, Gabrielle De Cuir, David Birney, Scott Brick, Jason Cole, Harlan Ellison, Christian Noble de Cuir, Don Schlossman, M. E. Willis, and Orson Scott Card. 2004. Macmillan Audio. ISBN: 9781427205261. 10.5 hrs. ♆ Ⓨ Ⓐ ♒

On a futuristic Earth and in space, Ender Wiggin proves himself—at least in the games he and his fellow students engage in—the best of the best in battling the hated Buggers. Until, that is, the games become all too real. Is it possible to win the war but lose the best of oneself? This mesmerizing production employs a large cast, including the author! Surprisingly, Rudnicki's lovely bass voice works well for the young Ender, while others fill in as his companions at the battle school, his siblings, and the untrustworthy adults. The power of the multiple voices enhances this classic science fiction tale, which is rich in action scenes but also in what science fiction does best—thoughtful exploration of moral, ethical, social, and intellectual issues.

Science Fiction; Coming-of-Age; Classic.

▶ **Hammett, Dashiell**
The Maltese Falcon. **Sam Spade Series.** Read by Michael Madsen, Sandra Oh, Edward Herrmann, Laura Gardner, Burt Ross, Michael Saad, Armin Shimerman, Keith Szarabajka, and Tom Towles. 2008. Blackstone. ISBN: 9781433252488. 3 hrs. ♉ 💱

One of Blackstone's Hollywood Theater of the Ear series, this audio dramatization, reminiscent of radio plays from the past, effectively adds sound effects to the sparse, precise language as voiced by a stellar cast. Madsen as Sam Spade fits Hammett's original description even better than Bogart's elegant movie portrayal, with a gravelly voice and cynical outlook that underlines the noir atmosphere of the book. As the scheming Brigid O'Shaughnessy, Oh alternates between wheedling and tears. Herrmann effortlessly switches between affability and sinister threats in his portrayal of Kasper Gutman. Absolutely riveting. For fans of the both the book and the movie.

Mystery; Classic.

Herbert, Frank
Dune. **Dune Series.** Read by Simon Vance, Euan Morton, Scott Brick, Orlagh Cassidy, John Ahlin, and Scott Sowers. 2007. BBC Audiobooks America. ISBN: 9780792748663. 21 hrs. ♉ 🏆 Y A 💱

The care taken with this production—a large cast of skilled narrators and evocative music scored throughout to underline dramatic scenes—speaks to the classic status of this benchmark science fiction novel, originally published in 1965. Vance's narration anchors the story with other cast members appearing throughout as individual characters. Spectacular narration, music, and other sound effects highlight this complex novel of political conspiracies, battle, and adventure as Paul, scion of the House of Atreides, comes of age and into his prophesied powers. As in all multinarrator readings, a cast list should have been provided by the publisher but wasn't.

Science Fiction; Adventure; Coming-of-Age; Classic.

Pullman, Philip
The Golden Compass. **His Dark Materials.** Read by Philip Pullman, Sean Barrett, Joanna Wyatt, Rupert Degas, Alison Dowling, Andrew Branch, Douglas Blackwell, Harriet Butler, Anna Cochlan, David Graham, Stephen Greif, Garrick Hagon, Andrew Lamont, Fiona Lamont, Alexander Mitchell, Arthur Mitchell, Hayward Morse, John O'Connor, Anne Rosenfeld, Liza Ross, Susan Sheridan, Jill Shilling, Stephen Thorne, and Rachel Wolf. 1999. Listening Library. ISBN: 0807210498. 10.8 hrs. ♉ Y A 💱

Fantasy novels are often timeless and ageless; this young adult title, the first in the series, pleases adult listeners as much as younger ones. With this full cast recording, Listening Library sets the standard for such performances. Music, sound effects, and spirited renditions are hallmarks of this production. Wedded with a provocative story line in a world filled with witches and armored beasts, along with more easily recognizable human characters paired with alter ego daemons, this becomes a contemporary fantasy classic. Twelve-year-old Lyra, educated at the colleges in Oxford, steals away on a life-altering adventure to the frozen north. Unlike many other recordings that simply list some of the narrators, the package conveniently gives a complete cast list.

Fantasy; Coming-of-Age.

Twice the Talent: Authors as Narrators

Almost any audiobook fan will quickly acknowledge that authors seldom make the best narrators. Authors generally aren't skilled readers, and no matter how engaging the story, they lack the ability to sustain a listener's interest for the length of the book. There are, however, a few exceptions. Generally speaking, authors make the best readers of their personal memoirs—they were there, after all—but sometimes they excel at other readings as well.

Delaney, Frank

Ireland: A Novel. Read by Frank Delaney. 2005. Harper Audio. ISBN: 9780060741891. 20 hrs.

Storyteller Delaney casts his spell over this historical novel, an exploration of Ireland's history told through a storyteller's craft and the tales he tells. Young Ronan, fascinated by an itinerant storyteller from his youth, searches for that man, and this quest leads him to his own past and future. Basic facts from Irish history vie with fascinating insights into the role of storytelling, as well as with meditations on the relationship between myth and history. Listening, of course, adds yet another level to this intriguing play on the art of the story, and natural storyteller that he is, Delaney excels as a narrator.

Historical Fiction.

▶ Gaiman, Neil

The Graveyard Book. Read by Neil Gaiman. 2008. Recorded Books. ISBN: 9781436158848. 7.5 hrs. ♉ ♛ ⓎⒶ

It comes as no surprise to fans that Gaiman's distinctive voice and cadence perfectly complement his edgy tale of a boy, orphaned as a baby, adopted by the denizens of a graveyard, and protected from those who want him dead by a vampire and a werewolf, among others. Gaiman's quirky humor resonates throughout, but this book also addresses a wide range of emotions, from fear to heartwarming pleasure. Each character—human, ghost, otherworldly being, good or bad—has a distinctive voice that reveals his nature. It's almost impossible to stop listening, especially as the suspense ratchets up at the end. Could another narrator read Gaiman's books? Probably, but perhaps not with equal care and pleasure in the words, images, and story.

Horror; Family Listening.

King, Stephen

On Writing: A Memoir of the Craft. Read by Stephen King. 2000. Recorded Books. ISBN: 0788751557. 8 hrs. Nonfiction. ♟ Y A

Although I am the first to argue that King should not record his own novels, I am an outspoken fan of this personal, practical, intimate guide to King, the person and the writer. No one else could convey his infectious passion for story and the hard-learned writing tips he offers. This is a practical guide as well as a powerful account of a man nearly destroyed by his demons who was saved by the redemptive power of writing. Earnest, evangelistic, and riveting, King's personal account should be required reading for teen fans and anyone who appreciates storytelling.

Memoir.

Kingsolver, Barbara

Prodigal Summer. Read by Barbara Kingsolver. 2001. Recorded Books. ISBN: 0788771825. 15 hrs. ⚓

Kingsolver's soft Southern cadence and clear emotional connection to people, place, and language make this an unforgettable listening experience. One can hear her pleasure in the wonders of nature and thus better understand her characters and the story. She imagines a small Appalachian community and the forces within, focusing on three characters and their lives: Park Service employee and loner Deanna Wolfe; Lusa Landowski, former city dweller, widowed and now tied to the land; and an aging organic farmer at odds with her equally elderly neighbor. Characters and issues drive this ecologically oriented tale, and Kingsolver presents all with a gentle touch and clear voice. Pure listening pleasure.

Literary Fiction; Women's Fiction.

Sedaris, David

Dress Your Family in Corduroy and Denim. Read by David Sedaris. 2004. Time Warner Audiobooks. ISBN: 1586215027. 6.5 hrs. Nonfiction. ♟ ♟

Once you have heard Sedaris perform his own work, you can hardly imagine anyone else succeeding at placing just the right sardonic emphasis. The written word barely stands up in comparison. His distinctive voice and deadpan delivery add an essential dimension to the humor and raise the audio productions of his book to performance art. These are mostly family stories—personal, detailed, quirky, and sometimes terrifyingly familiar—filled with flamboyant humor; they are not for the faint of heart. All his collections make excellent listening, but despite the fact that these are family stories, the language and content may restrict the audience to adults.

Humor; Memoir.

Trillin, Calvin

About Alice. Read by Calvin Trillin. 2006. Books on Tape. ISBN: 9781415935477. 1.5 hrs. Nonfiction.

Trillin's great affection for his wife and her integral role in his life are clear in all his writings. Here, in this homage to a dearly beloved companion, his voice echoes that tenderness, respect, and love, as he celebrates the life of an intelligent and wonderful woman, both muse and mother figure, an optimist who believed in family and education and was an outspoken advocate of both. Filled with anecdotes that are both humorous and touching, this elegantly written and heartwarming tribute explores a life well lived and the legacy left behind. Trillin, known for his deadpan delivery, brings the listener all the way into this deeply felt elegy, allowing the words to speak for themselves and create a lasting and affecting image.

Memoir; Biography.

Gone but Not Forgotten: Great Narrators Who Have Died

As listeners, we are always devastated when we lose favorite narrators. The narrators listed here left very deep impressions, and among those of us who appreciate stories well told, they won't be forgotten. If you haven't heard these narrators before, you might want to try these representative titles.

Kate Fleming/Anna Fields was an Audie winner and acclaimed narrator who read a range of both fiction and nonfiction and seemed always to capture the essence of characters and stories. She died tragically in 2006.

Patchett, Ann

Bel Canto. Read by Anna Fields. 2001. Blackstone Audio. ISBN: 0786197315. 12 hrs. ♛ ⬚

Through Fields's fabulous voice, every character lives in Patchett's award-winning novel. The premise: what happens to a group of wealthy, well-connected citizens of the world when terrorists interrupt a birthday party for a Japanese businessman in an unnamed South American country and hold the guests hostage for more than four months? The lyrical quality of Fields's voice and her skill with accents and vocal nuances heightens listeners' appreciation of the theme of the universality of music. Gorgeous language, complex characters, and a disturbing but thoughtful story are all enhanced by Fields's skill with voice and cadence.

Literary Fiction.

Frank Muller began his career in 1979 and was one of the industry's top narrators when he was critically injured in a motorcycle accident in 2002. He died in 2008, but he left a legacy of top-notch recordings, yet to be equaled. His distinctive cadence made him the perfect interpreter of dark, atmospheric stories, and he read any number of those across genres, from literary titles to horror.

▶ **King, Stephen**
The Shawshank Redemption. Read by Frank Muller. 1995. Penguin Audiobooks. ISBN: 9780143143956. 4.5 hrs.

 Muller may have been the finest narrator ever to perform King's novels, and this reading of the short story, "Rita Hayworth and the Shawshank Redemption," is one of his best. Muller's dark voice and precise cadence lend themselves to King's brooding novels and novellas. Here, he voices an inmate's struggle to survive—and escape—prison. Guards and fellow prisoners come to life as Muller's raw and edgy voice draws us in to the harsh realities of prison life. His powerful, riveting reading transforms the story, raising it to the sublime.

 Psychological Suspense.

Actress **Lynne Thigpen** was known as the premier reader of works by African American women, although she did not limit herself to these. Her first recording was Toni Morrison's *Jazz*, and her lyrical reading suited the musical style. She read much of Morrison's work as well as titles by Maya Angelou. She died suddenly in 2003.

Butler, Octavia E.
Parable of the Sower. **Parable Series.** Read by Lynne Thigpen. 2001. Recorded Books. ISBN: 9780788747601. 12 hrs. [Y][A] 📖

 This first book in Butler's Parable series takes place in 2025 in a Southern California on the verge of collapse. We learn the terrible details of the time through the diary of teenager Lauren Olamina who suffers from "hyperempathy," which forces her to feel the pain of others. Lauren escapes Los Angeles and travels with others, sowing her newfound religion called Earthseed. Thigpen reflects Lauren's despair and pain, as she chronicles her physical and emotional travails. Her heartfelt reading emphasizes the bleak tone of this acclaimed novel, which forecasts a dark future.

 Science Fiction; Classic.

Patrick Tull is perhaps best known for having recorded the entire Aubrey-Maturin series by Patrick O'Brian, but fans also remember his recordings of Ellis Peter's Brother Cadfael mysteries and Colin Dexter's mystery series featuring the irascible Inspector Morse. Tull died in 2006.

O'Brian, Patrick

Master and Commander. **Jack Aubrey and Stephen Maturin Series.** Read by Patrick Tull. 1991. Recorded Books. ISBN: 0788772015. 16.75 hrs.

Tull's interpretation of the characters and world of O'Brian's classic military adventure series set at sea is nothing short of sublime. His precise pronunciations and cadence reflect 19th-century speech patterns and vocabulary, and his wonderfully expressive voice, which switches readily from gravelly to soft and from Aubrey's jargon-rich military talk to Maturin's educated tones, makes listeners feel part of the adventure. O'Brian, of course, is the master of authentic historical detail from sailor's cant to naval actions. Author and narrator place listeners in the midst of battle and offer a glimpse into a fascinating friendship.

Adventure; Historical Fiction; Military Fiction.

It's a Man's World:
Compelling Male Narrators

There are dozens of great male voices in the world of audiobooks, and these are six of my favorites, listed along with a typical title. Argue if you like, but *you* try choosing the best!

Scott Brick. Although it may seem he has been typecast as a narrator of suspense/adventure/thrillers, Brick has also notably read science fiction, fantasy, occasional nonfiction, and even classics. He is known for subtle characterizations that capture personalities and his sense of the author's intent with both character and story.

Meltzer, Brad

The Book of Fate. Read by Scott Brick. 2006. Hachette Audio. ISBN: 9781594835452. 16 hrs.

Meltzer's suspenseful thriller provides an excellent stage for Brick's narrative strengths. Presidential assistant Wes Holloway has been injured, physically and emotionally, while protecting the president. He has survived, but now he realizes that someone is back to try again to harm the president. Plot twists, a Jeffersonian cipher, great behind-the-scenes politics and political chicanery, and a very real and sympathetic protagonist keep us on our toes until the really bad guys, imbued by Brick with a tangible sense of menace, show their stuff. Edge-of-the seat tension drives the pace of this memorable performance.

Thriller; Suspense; Adventure.

George Guidall. Readers easily recognize Guidall's distinctive voice; his gentle grandfatherly tones work well with children's books and gentle reads, but he can just as easily add an edge for thrillers and suspense. Guidall continues to please listeners across the genres, including comedy, drama, Westerns, and romance.

Hosp, David

Innocence. **Scott Finn Series.** Read by George Guidall. 2007. Recorded Books. ISBN: 9781428157323. 12.5 hrs.

Scott Finn catches a pro bono cold case and rediscovers his morality in this dark and dramatic legal thriller, the second featuring Finn. Guidall makes the most of the colorful material—a Salvadoran doctor set up for a crime as well as a legacy of police corruption and deadly danger for Finn and his associates. But there's also witty dialog and relentless pacing that never lags in Guidall's capable hands. His reading, especially his characterization of the multiple voices and accents and his clear investment in the compelling story, make a good book an excellent audiobook.

Legal Thriller.

Dick Hill. Although he has narrated fantasy, classics, popular fiction, biography, and general nonfiction, Hill is probably best known for reading gritty thrillers, novels of suspense, and mysteries. He narrates multiple series, and his distinctive cadence ratchets up the suspense and sustains the drama.

Deutermann, Peter T.

Nightwalkers. **Cam Richter Series.** Read by Dick Hill. 2009. Brilliance Audio. ISBN: 9781423336266. 12 hrs.

In this fourth adventure featuring North Carolina detective Cam Richter, Hill's Southern drawl perfectly suits the laconic policeman, who, tired of urban life, has bought a decaying plantation. But when Richter tries to move in with his German shepherds, he finds a host of eccentric neighbors and more than one ghost with deadly intentions. Hill's careful reading highlights the lovely descriptions while it establishes the sense of menace and builds it to the final twists.

Thriller; Mystery; Suspense.

John Lee. Lee's mesmerizing baritone evokes a multitude of moods from an affable Guernsey islander to a decidedly nervous witness to the eruption of Mt. Vesuvius, each appropriate to the story at hand. Lee has portrayed a range of characters in fiction and nonfiction, and his skill with South Asian accents makes him especially prized as a narrator of novels set in that area. His theatrical training guarantees both an expressive and authentic portrayal and a wonderful listening experience.

▶ **Pamuk, Orhan**

My Name Is Red. Read by John Lee. 2008. Books on Tape. ISBN: 9781415956861. 20.5 hrs. ♈ Ⓨ Ⓐ ☙

While Nobelist Pamuk's novel is a fascinating read, it is even better when heard, a credit to Lee's splendid narration of this murder mystery set in 16th-century Turkey at the time when Western artistic conventions were beginning to encroach on time-honored traditions. Each section is from a particular point of view: sometimes the perspective is that of the major players (the murdered miniaturist, his murderer, or the detective), and sometimes it is of non-humans and inanimate objects. Never mind the source of the voice, each receives individual treatment in Lee's animated performance. Listeners can hear his delight in the roles as he weaves stories within stories and maximizes Pamuk's playful style and language.

Literary Fiction; Historical Mystery; Historical Fiction; Fantasy.

Simon Prebble. Prebble seems always able to read with exactly the right tone and intensity. He presents characters and lets them and the story shine in the wide range of genres he has narrated: nonfiction, romance, literary fiction, fantasy, mystery, and thrillers, among others. He is also noted for his ability to convey emotional depths—from humor to passion—with aplomb.

Quinn, Julia

It's In His Kiss. **Bridgerton Series.** Read by Simon Prebble. 2006. Recorded Books. ISBN: 9781419382789. 10 hrs. ♈

This seventh title in Quinn's delightful Bridgerton series features the youngest daughter, Hyacinth, a vastly intelligent, witty, and charming Regency heroine who is too clever for the majority of gentlemen. That is, until she meets Gareth, grandson of the crotchety grande dame whom Hyacinth has befriended. Prebble elevates this entertaining romance with his plummy tones and wicked wit. The repartee scintillates and the sensual passages positively steam. Listeners can hear the laughter in his voice and are drawn inescapably into this entertaining romp.

Historical Romance; Humor.

Simon Vance. Praised for his amazing skill at characterization as well as accents, Vance has narrated more than 400 titles—nonfiction, classics, mystery, fantasy, science fiction, and more.

Novik, Naomi

His Majesty's Dragon. **Temeraire Series.** Read by Simon Vance. 2007. Books on Tape. ISBN: 9781415940143. 10 hrs.

In this first of Novik's alternate history series set during the Napoleonic Wars in a world where dragons live alongside men, Vance must voice dozens of characters from all over England and France, including hero and military man Will Laurence and his dragon Temeraire. He effortlessly transports listeners to this richly evoked world and makes it all believable.

Fantasy; Alternate History.

Let's Hear It from the Ladies: Engaging Female Narrators

These popular, critically acclaimed and award-winning narrators pop up throughout this book. Here they appear with titles that demonstrate their skill.

Barbara Caruso. Whether she is reading children's books, nonfiction, classics, or any of the wide range of fiction genres in which she has recorded, Caruso always brings a sense of style to her performance. She considers herself an interpreter of the author's words, and she strives to evoke the emotions within a text and to create vivid characters.

Binchy, Maeve

Evening Class. Read by Barbara Caruso. 2000. Recorded Books. ISBN: 9781419321344. 15.5 hrs.

Binchy's diverse collection of characters provides the perfect canvas for Caruso's artistry. A Dublin-based adult education Italian class, taught by a woman who followed her lover to Sicily years earlier, attracts an unappreciated Latin teacher, along with other Dubliners of all ages and classes who simply want to explore another culture. Caruso's performance elevates the characters and their dreams, building on Binchy's heartwarming story while providing distinctive personalities for each.

Women's Fiction; Gentle Reads.

Bernadette Dunne. Dunne's impressive talent lends itself to a wide range of recordings, from the lyrical prose of Richard Powers's *The Echo Maker* to the intense suspense and emotional turmoil of Iris Johansen's titles. Whether she is reading historical fiction, mysteries, inspirational fiction, or nonfiction, she brings the appropriate tone and exposes the emotional intensity or underlying humor of titles.

Weisberger, Lauren

The Devil Wears Prada. Read by Bernadette Dunne. 2003. Books on Tape. ISBN: 0736693378. 15 hrs.

Before we had Meryl Streep, Anne Hathaway, and Emily Blunt, we had Bernadette Dunne, whose polished reading of this exposé of the fashion world introduced many listeners to the delights of this story about the bad boss and the naive employee who triumphs in the end. Deliciously catty dialog and bigger-than-life characters enhance this spot-on interpretation of life in the very fast lane. Dunne comfortably projects the put-upon assistant as readily as the snarky boss, and her performance makes the most of the humor that pervades the novel.

Women's Fiction; Chick Lit; Humor.

Katherine Kellgren. Kellgren seems to have burst on the recording scene with her splendid performances narrating L.A. Meyer's Bloody Jack adventures, a series of flamboyant and adventurous historical novels for youth starring the epony-mous "Jack," who is really a young woman. Her trademark energy, enthusiasm, and skill with accents have made her a prized narrator for a wide range of books featuring young women as protagonists.

Grahame-Smith, Seth, and Jane Austen
Pride and Prejudice and Zombies. Read by Katherine Kellgren. 2009. Brilliance Audio. ISBN: 9781441816764. 10.5 hrs.

How better to bring a classic title up to date than by adding zombies? First among the zombie/classic craze, this expanded version brings zombie mayhem to the quiet byways of rural 19th-century England, with Elizabeth Bennett and her sisters among the foremost zombie slayers. Kellgren's tone allows Austen's novel to shine while providing the perfect tongue-in-cheek hauteur to sustain the wildly amusing interspersions of the zombie invasion and battles. She gives us all the familiar characters—and updates the familiar tale with a little twist.

Classic; Humor.

Davina Porter. From histories, biographies, classic novels, and historical fiction to contemporary mysteries and psychological suspense, Porter has made a name for herself as a mesmerizing and flawless interpreter of character and language. Although she is probably best known as the narrator of Diana Gabaldon's lengthy historical novels, she is also familiar to fans of Alexander McCall Smith, Anne Perry, M.C. Beaton, Ruth Rendell, Philippa Gregory, and others.

McCall Smith, Alexander
The Sunday Philosophy Club. **Isabel Dalhousie Series.** Read by Davina Porter. 2004. Recorded Books. ISBN: 1402590628. 9.25 hrs.

In this first book in the series featuring Isabel Dalhousie, Scottish philosopher and amateur detective Isabel witnesses a young man plummet to his death and feels obligated to investigate, with the assistance, of course, of her intriguingly eccentric fellow philosophers. Porter excels at creating a multitude of characters and precise Scottish accents to fix each firmly by class and background. Her portrayal of the somewhat dithering Isabel brings a touch of humor and endless charm to this delightful series.

Mystery; Humor.

Kate Reading. Alone and with her husband Michael Kramer, Reading has built a reputation as a narrator of science fiction and fantasy titles, although her repertoire extends beyond that narrow focus to include historical fiction, classics, mysteries, and nonfiction. She has recorded all of Patricia Cornwell's Kay Scarpetta mysteries as well as Carolyn G. Hart's Death on Demand series. Her readings create believable characters, whatever the setting, and voices that reflect period styles and geographic regions.

▶ **Willis, Connie**

Bellwether. Read by Kate Reading. 2009. Blackstone Audio. ISBN: 9781433246241. 6.5 hrs. ⚇

    I always thought this classic Willis tale, which combines intellect with wit and romance, was the perfect airplane read: engaging yet provocative. Now I'm willing to add that it's the perfect airplane listen, with Reading's delightful portrayal of the collision of the worlds of fad and science within the laws of chaos theory. Reading brings just the right human touch to scientist Sandra Foster and her search for the origin of fads, while she evokes the quintessential airhead in Flip, who stirs up chaos within the lab where Sandra works. Willis, ably aided by Reading, brings all the disparate elements together to create romantic comedy with a very interesting twist.

    Science Fiction; Humor; Romance.

Barbara Rosenblat. Known as the queen of accents, Rosenblat is the go-to narrator when an audiobook requires precision or a variety of voices. She also narrates more series than one might imagine—titles by Lisa Scottoline, Nevada Barr, Elizabeth Peters, Diane Mott Davidson, and more—and yet she makes each character individual and each story unforgettable.

Fairstein, Linda A.

Final Jeopardy. **Alexandra Cooper Novels.** Read by Barbara Rosenblat. 2007. Recorded Books. ISBN: 9781402570797. 10.5 hrs.

    Rosenblat brings her prodigious skill with accents to bear in this first entry in a long-running legal thriller series, capturing the voices of various New Yorkers including series protagonists Assistant District Attorney Alexandra Cooper and policemen Mercer Wallace and Mike Chapman. Here, Cooper investigates the murder of a friend who was staying in her Martha's Vineyard retreat. Was she to have been the intended victim? New Yorker Rosenblat also reflects Fairstein's love of the city, its landmarks and traditions, and its denizens, native and immigrant alike. Each title in this compelling series delves deeply into the city and its fascinating history and landmarks.

    Thriller.

A Literary Gazetteer: Well Written and Well Spoken

Well performed audio highlights the best of literary fiction. The gorgeous prose, whether lush or spare; intriguing characters; and provocative story lines translate well to audio. This admittedly quirky collection of titles proves the point.

▶ **Clinch, Jon**

Finn. Read by Ed Sala. 2007. Recorded Books. ISBN: 9781428124462. 11.25 hrs. 🏆 📚

Did you ever wonder about Huckleberry Finn's notorious father? With looping flashbacks and elegant language reminiscent of Twain's own, Clinch takes us back to the 1830s and fills in the details. Characters familiar from Twain's tale as well as new ones people this novel of racial issues and murder. Sala's expert narration of this vivid re-imagining of Twain's world takes readers back to another time and place. His voice captures the characters completely, and his measured pace allows the rich language to seep into our consciousness. Clinch clearly wrote this to be read aloud, and Sala brings the story to life.

Literary Fiction; Historical Fiction.

Jin, Ha

A Free Life. Read by Jason Ma. 2007. BBC Audiobooks America. ISBN: 9780792750437. 22 hrs. 📚

In his first book set outside China, Jin explores the immigrant experience in this layered tale of Nan Wu who brings his wife and son to America to escape increased oppression in China. In polished, spare prose and with a pointillist's eye for detail, Jin examines how families make their way in a new culture, socially and politically, and how this particular family transitions from being Chinese immigrants to Chinese Americans. Ma's masterful reading reveals this acculturation, as hesitations in his cadence and a distinct Chinese accent give way to only a slight accent as the acclimation of the characters progresses. A character-centered novel rich in provocative intellectual and domestic themes.

Literary Fiction; Multicultural Fiction.

Lively, Penelope

Consequences. Read by Josephine Bailey. 2007. Tantor Media. ISBN: 9781400135028. 9 hrs. 📚

Three generations of women drive this heartwarming story. Orphaned Ruth becomes interested in her family history. She follows it back to her grandparents and to her artist grandfather's illustrations on the walls of their cottage and the wood engravings he left before he was sent to fight in Crete, where he died in 1941. Bailey's intimate tones enliven these thoughtful, engaging characters, while her stylish interpretation gives full voice to the elegant and graceful language. Her reading enhances the lovely, elegiac tone of this provocative exploration of the nature of family legacies.

Literary Fiction; Family Saga.

Munro, Alice

Runaway. Read by Kymberly Dakin. 2004. BBC Audiobooks America. ISBN: 0792733673. 11 hrs. 🎧 🏆

Although I don't often read short stories, I do enjoy listening to really good ones—and these are just that. These award-winning, timeless tales focus on small-town and rural Canadian women at various points in their lives. Evocative, introspective, and haunting, these long short stories delve into the psychological as well as the mundane. Dakin's reading of Munro's sublime prose highlights its graceful austerity. She captures the darker mood of most of the stories, and her understated reading allows characters and Munro's glorious language to speak for themselves.

Literary Fiction.

Murakami, Haruki

After Dark. Read by Janet Song. 2007. Books on Tape. ISBN: 9781415938591. 5.75 hrs. 📚

This snapshot of Tokyo at night portrays lonely, disenfranchised characters making connections, if for only one evening. It is set against a surreal landscape that seems surprisingly authentic. In her role as omniscient narrator, Song directs the action and our perspective, much like the narrator of a 19th-century novel. Her lovely voice, accented in Chinese and Japanese, reflects the characters and their cadences, as it also invokes the jazz rhythms that shape the haunting, lyrical prose. Seductive and magical.

Literary Fiction.

One Story, Many Voices: Multiple Narrators

In these novels multiple narrators read sections of a book told from their character's point of view. Yet each must also voice all the characters who speak in that section. This setup requires skilled narrators to make it work.

Gardner, Lisa

The Neighbor. **Detective D. D. Warren Series.** Read by Emily Jane Card, Kirby Heyborne, and Kirsten Potter. 2009. Books on Tape. ISBN: 9781415963166. 13.5 hrs.

Gardner's compelling tale of a young woman who disappears lends itself to multiple narrators. Was she murdered by her husband? Was she kidnapped by the convicted child-molester neighbor? The book is designed to present various points of view, and Card and Potter divide the female voices of investigating police detective D. D. Warren and the missing Sandy Jones, while Heyborne voices the haunted sex offender. Employing a mix of first- and third-person narration, the plot gallops along, with listeners brought up short with cliffhanger chapter endings and questions that remain unanswered until the very end. Secrets and secret lives, past and present, and a sense that not one of the affected characters is quite what he seems add to the nightmare tone. Enough investigation to please mystery fans and a growing sense of foreboding and danger-just-around-the-corner to please suspense fans.

Suspense; Mystery.

Maine, David

The Preservationist. Read by Tyler Bunch, Wendy Hoopes, Clayton Barclay Jones, John Randolph Jones, Jenna Lamia, David Pittu, Maggi-Meg Reed, and Barbara Rosenblat. 2004. HighBridge Audio. ISBN: 1565118715. 6.5 hrs. ☜

Maine's retelling of the story of the flood from Genesis is both comic and very human, made even more delightful and real by the large cast who perform as Noe (aka Noah), his wife, his three grown sons, and their own wives. Needless to say both human and animal menageries generate difficulties for Noe, as each human has a voice, and uses it, giving the large cast plenty of space to showcase their skills. As each character expresses concerns and opinions, adding layer upon layer to the bare bones of the story as we know it, the listener's pleasure grows. From the curmudgeonly Noe—he is, after all, 600 years old—to daughter-in-law Ilya's persistent questioning of the purpose of all this trouble, Maine and the cast of characters enliven this familiar Bible story.

Literary Fiction; Humor.

▶ **Stockett, Kathryn**

The Help. Read by Bahni Turpin, Octavia Spencer, Jenna Lamia, and Cassandra Campbell. 2009. Books on Tape. ISBN: 9781415961254. 18 hrs. ☗ ♈ ☜

This first novel lends itself to multiple narrators, with sections set out in specific voices to provide a character's take on events. Eugenia "Skeeter" Phelan returns from college to hometown Jackson, Mississippi, in 1962, a naive, budding writer who wants to tell stories that get her ostracized by her white peers. After all, who would want to read about the lives of the maids? These richly detailed lives, written in musical speech that sings in the listener's ears, create an authentic, heartwarming novel of the civil rights movement, beautifully told.

Literary Fiction; Historical Fiction; Women's Fiction.

Vreeland, Susan

Girl in Hyacinth Blue. Read by Loren Lester, Sheryl Bernstein, Martin Ferrero, Gigi Bermingham, Jennifer Baum, J. D. Cullum, Tom Fitzpatrick, and Janellen Steininger. 2001. HighBridge Audio. ISBN: 1565115449. 5 hrs. ☜

Vreeland's compelling tale of a Vermeer painting traces the painting's provenance, moving backward in time from the present day to the 17th century, thus exploring Dutch cultural and social history. Each section provides a snapshot of the particular period and reveals how the painting affected the lives of the owners. The multiple readers highlight both Vreeland's lyrical prose and Vermeer's image-rich style.

Literary Fiction; Historical Fiction; Art; Social History.

Weir, Alison

Innocent Traitor. Read by Davina Porter, Gerald Doyle, Bianca Amato, Jenny Sterlin, and Stina Nielsen. 2007. Recorded Books. ISBN: 9781423390343. 18.25 hrs.

A dark, foreboding tone sets the stage early on in this dramatic historical novel of Lady Jane Gray, great niece of England's Henry VIII and a Protestant political pawn who was placed on the throne after Edward's death to prevent Catholic Mary from ascending. Although it is Jane's story, voiced by Nielsen, the complex novel interweaves voices and viewpoints from other interested parties in order to present extensive historical detail and political machinations. Stellar performances from a distinguished cast add depth to these historical figures caught in this dramatic political conflict between Catholics and Protestants.

Historical Fiction; Royalty.

Unique Voices: Characters You Never Expected to Hear

Sometimes the central characters of stories are so unusual that they affect our perceptions of the story itself, allowing us to see events from their distinctly different points of view. It takes great skill on the part of the narrator to translate such a unique voice in audio, but in each of these titles, that is just what happens, allowing listeners to focus on the voice and viewpoint of a singular central character.

Bradley, Alan

The Sweetness at the Bottom of the Pie. **Buckshaw Chronicles.** Read by C. Alan Entwistle. 2009. Books on Tape. ISBN: 9781415964484. 10 hrs. ♛ Y A

Precocious 11-year-old Flavia de Luce is drawn into mysterious happenings when a dead bird is left at her small-town English home. When she finds a body in the garden and her father is arrested for murder, she becomes fully involved in the investigation, employing science, literature, and intuition to propel the denouement. Entwistle clearly relishes the role of "Flavia the Investigator," as well as "Flavia the Pest," whose experiments with poisons menace her older sister's sanity and peace of mind. The engaging narrator opens a window on English life in the 1950s from a fresh and clever perspective.

Mystery; Humor.

Haddon, Mark

The Curious Incident of the Dog in the Night-Time. Read by Jeff Woodman. 2003. Recorded Books. ISBN: 9781402559808. 6.25 hrs. ♛ ⛨ Y A

If the book is accounted a marvel, the audio version is so much more. Woodman captures 15-year-old Christopher Boone perfectly with his precise, ordered sentences and flat emotions. Christopher suffers from Asperger's syndrome, a form of autism, and while his emotional life may be blunted, this math genius explores the world in ways both unique and unexpected. Ostensibly a mystery—he seeks to discover who killed the neighbor's dog—it is also a unique glimpse into Christopher's mind, as chapters alternate between the investigations and ruminations on the nature of life and the universe. The novel contains some drawings, which Woodman describes vividly, and his portrayal of the tale is so expert that listeners will not feel they have missed a thing.

Literary Fiction; Coming-of-Age.

Quinn, Spencer
Dog On It. **Chet and Bernie Series.** Read by Jim Frangione. 2009. Recorded Books. ISBN: 9781436171977. 9.75 hrs. Ⓨ Ⓐ

Divorced ex-cop, down-on-his-luck Bernie Little may run the struggling Little Detective Agency, but his endearing mutt Chet, a police K9 dropout, gives it its special élan. Together—and apart—they investigate a mystery involving a missing teenager and the Russian mafia, but the real charm of this book, the first in a projected series, is Chet's very appealing and truly canine point of view. Frangione meets the challenge of voicing a dog's viewpoint with a breathless urgency, as Chet moves quickly from point to point, easily diverted from his train of thought by endless distractions. It's Chet's absolute dogginess that makes this work, combined with smart dialog, humor, danger, and the clear affection between Chet and Bernie. Although Chet's voice dominates, Frangione gets to show off his skill with voices and accents for the likeable Bernie, the Russian baddies, and a cast of others, good and bad, who add to the mayhem.

Mystery; Humor.

Sebold, Alice
The Lovely Bones. Read by Alyssa Bresnahan. 2002. Recorded Books. ISBN: 1402540558. 11.75 hrs. 🏆 Ⓨ Ⓐ 📖

In the first sentence of this book, listeners learn that heroine Susie Salmon was raped and stabbed to death and that she is recounting her story from Heaven. Bresnahan embodies this unexpectedly eloquent young victim, expressing her regrets but also voicing her understanding of a life well lived, despite its brevity. Her rich, gorgeous voice captures the teenagers as well as the adults whom Susie observes from afar. An emotionally charged story and a reading that enhances and transforms the written words to create an intimate connection between character and audience.

Literary Fiction; Coming-of-Age.

▶ **Wroblewski, David**
The Story of Edgar Sawtelle. Read by Richard Poe. 2008. Recorded Books. ISBN: 9781436149587. 21.5 hrs. 🏆 Ⓨ Ⓐ 📖

Few challenges seem as great as narrating a book told by a mute protagonist. In the print version, different typefaces indicate unusual styles, but in an audio format, the task falls on the narrator to translate the visual cues of the book into sound. Poe succeeds by subtly altering his deep voice, flattening the narration to reflect the mute boy. But that may be the least of Poe's challenges in this richly re-imagined retelling of Hamlet, with young Edgar assisted by his family's dogs in uncovering his uncle Claude's perfidy. Almondine, the dog who has been Edgar's constant companion since his birth, must also be voiced. And then there's the ghost of Edgar's dead father. Darkly foreboding, tragic yet heartwarming, this tale's graceful language and atmosphere are enhanced by a splendid reading.

Literary Fiction; Coming-of-Age.

Phonetic Genius: Virtuoso Performances

Whether they are saddled with a huge cast of characters or a plot so twisted that only the best could keep us from being confused or a difficult style, these narrators provide virtuoso performances as they tell us interesting stories.

Clarke, Susanna

Jonathan Strange & Mr. Norrell. Read by Simon Prebble. 2004. BBC/Audiobooks America. ISBN: 0792735315. 32 hrs. ♛ 📚

In an alternate 19th-century England where magic still exists, Mr. Norrell claims to be the last magician standing, and to prove that, he performs feats of magic and claims the power to defeat Napoleon. When his student, Jonathan Strange, begins to surpass him, the battle between the two magicians is joined. Myriad characters, all believably and individually portrayed, lyrical prose, and smart dialog vie with multiple shifts in scene and a complex style that would make this a nightmare for a less skilled narrator. Prebble, however, handles all with ease, including the extensive and often amusing footnotes that fill the book. Exhilarating and simply irresistible.

Fantasy; Alternate History; Humor.

▶ Gaiman, Neil

Anansi Boys. Read by Lenny Henry. 2005. BBC/Audiobooks America. ISBN: 0792737830. 10 hrs. ♛ Ⓨ Ⓐ

Audio may be the perfect way to appreciate this heartwarming fantasy and Gaiman's wonderful use of language and description. When his father dies, hero Fat Charlie Nancy discovers he has a brother, Spider, who steals his girl and tricks him into losing his job. Spider is, in fact, the West African trickster hero, here to make Fat Charlie's life a misery. Henry navigates the wealth of quirky, curious, likeable characters with ease, switching seamlessly among British, American, Caribbean, and African accents, not to mention the voices of the gods whom Fat Charlie hopes to enlist to fight Spider. In this story propelled by intriguing folktales and music of the Caribbean, Fat Charlie eventually discovers his true self, and listeners understand that they have experienced a remarkable example of storytelling perfection.

Fantasy; Humor.

Lethem, Jonathan
Motherless Brooklyn. Read by Frank Muller. 2001. Recorded Books. ISBN: 9781402510564. 10 hrs. ♛ ➽

Among his other problems, Lionel Essrog has Tourette's syndrome, and the spasms, twitches, and nonsensical (often profane) outbursts make him a problematical character to be telling his own story. Muller is at the top of his game in his wonderfully effective depiction of this unstable protagonist. He moves effortlessly from the normal Lionel to Lionel in the throes of Tourette's, when his voice flattens and races as he speaks uncontrollably. While the performance may be confusing and even irritating at first, it is ultimately fascinating and even enjoyable, as listeners simply settle in for the ride. The story, by the way, revolves around Lionel's investigation to discover the murderer of his mentor, a small-time hood.

Literary Fiction; Mystery.

Rowling, J. K.
Harry Potter and the Sorcerer's Stone. **Harry Potter Series.** Read by Jim Dale. 1999. Listening Library. ISBN: 0807286001. 8 hrs. ⛎ ♛ Ⓨ Ⓐ ➽

Start here, even if you have read the entire series, and sit back and enjoy Dale's pitch-perfect interpretation of the vast cast of characters and endless plot machinations. Marketed originally for children, this is a fantasy series for all ages and one for families to enjoy, even though the later titles become darker. Dale is cited in *The Guinness Book of World Records* for having created more than 200 individual voices for the series, but that he ages his characters' voices through the seven years of their training—and the series—makes his achievement all the more impressive. In this first volume, orphan Harry is sent to Hogwarts School of Witchcraft and Wizardry to claim his heritage and battle the dark lord. Action and adventure, magic spells, the arcane rules of quidditch, and the power of friendships and love create a magical series, all of which Dale conveys through nuances, pitch, pauses, and meticulous narration.

Fantasy; Humor; Family Listening.

Wolfe, Tom
Bonfire of the Vanities. Read by Joe Barrett. 2009. Blackstone Audiobooks. ISBN: 9781433288418. 27.5 hrs.

Whatever the impetus behind Blackstone's new recording of Wolfe's classic New York City tale, this is a title for our times, what with the financial collapse and the popularity of the television series *Mad Men.* Barrett's reading elevates Wolfe's verbal skewering of people, institutions, and beliefs to a fine art. Convincing accents and cadences identify each character in the large cast, as he slyly evokes the underlying humor and captures every nuance in this scathing exposé of the power, politics, and greed among the rich and disdainful. Relive the worst of New York in the 1980s—and enjoy every gloriously gruesome minute! Wolfe's literary tour de force lives on in this splendid audio version.

Literary Fiction; Humor.

Chapter Two

Mood

Mood is an area in which audiobooks excel—or fail miserably. Good narrators reflect and enhance the mood established by the author. The mood may be comic or serious; it may project building sexual tension or suspense; it may convey a comfortable feeling or keep the listener on edge. Whatever its nature, mood plays the role of a movie soundtrack and sets the stage for the listening experience.

Mood in audiobooks works slightly differently from that in books, as the narrator's voice is crucial in establishing the mood. In a humorous romance, for example, we are able to hear the laughter in the narrator's voice during witty repartee. In suspense, thrillers, and mysteries, the dread in the character's voice as he faces danger should be audible, even tangible. In horror tales narrators take us inside the haunted protagonist's mind, then suddenly terrify us with aural manifestations of evil. And in any genre, listeners can recognize the affection of one character for another simply from the way the narrator reads, even before the plot affirms it. If the story is told tongue-in-cheek or the action is intentionally over-the-top, we hear this in the narrator's voice. Narrators direct our impressions, and if their reading is off—deadpan when it should be animated, for example—the book and our listening experience suffer.

These lists identify popular moods and offer listening suggestions to match them.

Sleepless Nights: Stories with Haunting Atmospheres

It's a shame that more horror novels and short stories are not available in audio versions, as many seem written to be heard out loud. The moody tale, filled with dangerous and haunted characters, inspires our imaginations to work overtime, and hearing these stories seems to revive long ago memories of telling ghost stories around the campfire, until every sound is magnified, and everyone is too frightened to sleep.

Gout, Leopoldo

Ghost Radio. Read by Pedro Pascal. 2008. Harper Audio. ISBN: 9780061661570. 8.5 hrs.

Gabriel and Joaquin become friends after a freak car accident kills their families. Their adolescent pranks take them to an abandoned radio station, where another accident occurs, leaving Gabriel dead. Or is he? In this menacing tale, reminiscent of *Twilight Zone* episodes, the radio becomes a portal between the worlds of the living and dead. Pascal's reading underlines the building terror and general creepiness of the novel, playing up the emotional range through the different points of view and a time line that jumps from past to present, dream to reality, leaving listeners dangling, unsettled, and caught up in the nightmare. While the audio lacks the disturbing illustrations featured in the book, it more than makes up for them with the moody performance.

Horror.

▶ Hill, Joe

Heart-Shaped Box. Read by Stephen Lang. 2007. Books on Tape. ISBN: 9781415937556. 11 hrs. ♗ ♚

Judas Coyne, a heavy metal superstar now in retirement, collects obscure, macabre objects. But the ghost he buys over the Internet turns out to be the spirit of his late girlfriend's stepfather—and he's very real and out for revenge! The creepiness of this atmospheric story gradually uncoils, as Coyne takes to the road to escape. Lang's reading blends the supernatural with the realistic in ways that increase the menace and growing uneasiness and reveal the horror of the everyday blown up to nightmare proportions.

Horror; Thriller.

King, Stephen

Just after Sunset. Read by Stephen King, Jill Eikenberry, Holter Graham, George Guidall, Ron McLarty, Denis O'Hare, Ben Shenkman, Skipp Sudduth, Mare Winningham, and Karen Ziemba. 2008. Recorded Books. ISBN: 9781436178297. 15 hrs. ♚ Ⓨ Ⓐ

Fans of King's haunting, atmospheric novels sometimes forget what a fabulous short-story writer he is—until a new collection comes out. All these earthy, nightmare tales display undercurrents of the macabre, but some are more psychological while others offer horror readers visceral details. Since it might have been difficult for one reader to sustain the atmospheric tone and highlight the particular menace of each story in this diverse collection, there is a large cast of readers, each reading a story or two. Even King himself gets his chance to read, and his Maine accent and laid-back approach work perfectly for "Harvey's Dream." 🏆

Horror.

Poe, Edgar Allan

The Edgar Allan Poe Audio Collection. Read by Vincent Price and Basil Rathbone. 2000. Caedmon. ISBN: 9780694524198. 6 hrs.

This delightful collection of some of Poe's best poems and stories offers positively chilling readings by classic horror masters Vincent Price and Basil Rathbone. From "The Pit and the Pendulum" and "The Tell-Tale Heart" to "The Cask of Amontillado" and "Annabel Lee," these poems and tales may be familiar and frequently recorded, but these performances stand out. Even those unfamiliar with these actors' stentorian tones will recognize their dramatic skill and their ability to transcend the decades and bring these stories and poems to vibrant life once again. One small quibble: neither narrator gives the title of each piece, requiring listeners to follow the table of contents. Otherwise, these are sure to unnerve even the most stalwart listener.

Horror; Classic.

Ransom, Christopher

The Birthing House. Read by Edward Herrmann. 2009. Blackstone. ISBN: 9781433289224. 10 hrs.

This gripping haunted house tale is all about mood, and Herrmann excels at ratcheting up the nightmare tension from Conrad Harrison's discovery of the perfect home to his realization that he is now trapped by the home and the spirits it holds. The house in question was a home for unwed mothers, run by a psychotic doctor, and the spirits of the denizens now cry out, day and night, and even materialize, as possession becomes their goal. Creepy with plenty of twists, this compelling tale will raise the hair on the back of any listener's neck. Herrmann's carefully calibrated narration makes the growing sense of dread inescapable.

Horror.

Curl Up in Your Easy Chair:
Comfortable Listening

Some stories create an experience of pure satisfaction—they leave us feeling good. Mood may be bittersweet or uplifting, but the end result is stories that leave us with a sigh of contentment when they end.

Allen, Sarah Addison
The Sugar Queen. Read by Karen White. 2008. Books on Tape. ISBN: 9781415954331. 8 hrs. ♛

Josey Cirrini has always lived in her mother's shadow, caring for her but living a secret life with candy bars and romance novels in her closet—until Della Lee Baker invades that life, camps in her closet, and compels Josey to take charge of her own future. A sprinkling of wit, humor, and romance, as well as just a touch of magic, enhances this charming and timeless story of family relationships. With her seductively soft Southern drawl, White captures the tone of the book well and inhabits each of the quirky characters. Her pleasure in the unraveling of secrets and events is infectious. From Josey and her innocent wonder, to her demanding mother, to the larger-than-life Della, and Della's loathsome boyfriend, the characters and their innermost thoughts become clear through White's empathetic delivery of this lighthearted novel that addresses issues of the heart.

Coming-of-Age; Gentle Reads; Women's Fiction.

▶ **Binchy, Maeve**
Heart and Soul. 2009. Read by Sile Bermingham. 2009. Books on Tape. ISBN: 9781415960271. 15.25 hrs.

This novel centers on a clinic for cardiac care, but Binchy's true focus, as always, is on her characters; she intertwines the lives of patients, staff, and their families with those of familiar friends from previous titles. Bermingham shades her lilting Irish accent to depict a cast filled predominantly with Dubliners, and her (and Binchy's) affection for the characters resonates in her performance. Bermingham effortlessly evokes those elements that make this a quintessential Binchy tale: the charming, timeless story of relationships—family, friends, and lovers—that is upbeat in tone and narrated with warmth and good humor.

Gentle Reads; Women's Fiction.

Chiaverini, Jennifer
The Quilter's Apprentice. **Elm Creek Quilts.** Read by Christina Moore. 2004. Recorded Books. ISBN: 1402575254. 8.5 hrs.

This is the first in the long-running series—all read by Moore—of gentle tales of quilting and women's lives. It's a heartwarming tale of an unlikely friendship between the crotchety Mrs. Compson, back in Elm Creek after her sister's death, and a young woman looking for more in her life. They grow together, and their friendship and quilting help them sort out life's difficulties. Moore provides individual voices for the main characters and other continuing characters in later volumes. Her distinctive almost scratchy voice and warm tones are the perfect complement to these often moving stories, rich in characters and quilting lore.

Gentle Reads; Women's Fiction.

Ross, Ann B.
Miss Julia Meets Her Match. **Miss Julia Series.** Read by Claudia Hughes. 2004.
BBC Audiobooks America. ISBN: 0792732332. 10.75 hrs.

Miss Julia's spunk and Southern charm seem to go hand in hand with the whole idea of comfortable reads. One can start anywhere in this delightful series and fall right in step with the quirky characters, the gossipy North Carolina town, and the relaxed pace. In this episode, Miss Julia, a widow on the far side of 70, wrangles with outsiders who want to build a religious theme park just outside town and puts off persistent suitor Sam until all is resolved. A bevy of narrators have read titles in the Miss Julia series, but Hughes brings a special charm and the right combination of wit and sass that embodies the unique personality of this forthright and unflappable widow.

Gentle Reads; Women's Fiction; Humor.

Sparks, Nicholas
The Lucky One. Read by John Bedford Lloyd. 2008. Books on Tape. ISBN: 9781415959664. 10.5 hrs.

Logan considers himself lucky to have survived three tours of duty in Iraq, and he credits a picture he found of an unknown young woman with his luck. Determined to find the girl, he walks from Colorado to North Carolina, searching for her. But will his luck hold? Does he deserve love, and will she be the woman of his dreams? Lloyd sets the stage for this gentle, heartfelt story from the very first with his soft, deep voice and down-home accent. Even Logan's war memories and the troubles he and Elizabeth, the young woman from the photograph, face barely ruffle the smooth flow and timeless feel of this poignant tale.

Gentle Reads.

Don't Look Now: Dark and Disturbing

While readers can certainly apprehend the darker tone in many novels as they read, listeners have the advantage: atmospheric novels on audio resonate with that uneasy sense that danger lurks. Haunting qualities of the edgy prose, realized through the voices of expert narrators, dominate the listener's sense of the story. There seems to be no escape from the imminent danger.

▶ **Barker, Clive**
Coldheart Canyon: A Hollywood Ghost Story. Read by Frank Muller. 2001.
Harper Collins. ISBN: 0694526630. 22 hrs. 🎧

From Hollywood's Coldheart Canyon, where the disturbingly evocative prologue is set, to the obscure Romanian village in the 1920s where a glamorous star was born and raised, this chilling tale documents Hollywood Babylon and the ghosts that dwell there still, awaiting fresh prey. After a botched plastic surgery operation, modern day star Todd Pickett retreats to an isolated Hollywood mansion to recover, only to discover the 1920s stars and glamour live on in the mansion and feed on those foolish enough to enter. Violence abounds as terror builds. Muller's voice is particularly suited to this story and genre. He builds tension step-by-step, suggesting the darker meaning that lurks behind the words, and creates a disturbing atmosphere of unease.

Horror; Fantasy.

Cain, Chelsea

HeartSick. **Archie and Gretchen Series.** Read by Carolyn McCormick. 2007. BBC Audiobooks America. ISBN: 9780792750222. 10.5 hrs.

McCormick's reading of this visceral novel of psychological suspense and serial murder disturbs even as it seduces. Portland detective Archie Sheridan brought serial murderer Gretchen Lowell to justice, but not before she tortured and nearly killed him, yet he remains in her thrall. When another serial murderer appears on the scene, Sheridan turns to Lowell for help reading the clues, only to be drawn into her net again. Relentless pacing, smart dialog, and a chilling tone make this an unforgettable tale of obsession, a trip to the dark side of the heart and mind.

Suspense; Psychological Suspense; Thriller.

Ellory, R. J.

A Quiet Belief in Angels. Read by Mark Bramhall. 2009. Blackstone Audiobooks. ISBN: 9781441722423. 15.4 hrs.

Haunted by the murder of young girls in his rural Georgia community in the 1940s, Joseph Vaughan and his friends form "The Guardians" to try to protect their community. Their failure—the grisly murders continue—haunts Vaughan for the next 50 years, until he finally identifies and confronts the murderer. Bramhall's measured reading captures the elegant, layered prose and intensifies the evocative, brooding tone. Listeners relate to the powerful, intimate character study as well as to Vaughan's quest for justice.

Psychological Suspense; Mystery; Literary Fiction; Coming-of-Age.

McCarthy, Cormac

No Country for Old Men. Read by Tom Stechschulte. 2005. Recorded Books. ISBN: 1419344587. 7.5 hrs. ♉

McCarthy's lyrical yet violent tale of the modern West offers graceful language and deadly encounters. While out hunting Llewelyn Moss stumbles on a drug transfer gone bad and helps himself to the abandoned spoils. He takes the money and runs, only to find out that he is now being pursued by a relentless psychopathic killer. Stechschulte's unforgettable performance reflects the dramatic events in a measured pace and contrasts the gorgeous prose against the menacing tone and grisly violence. Sheriff Tom Bell, cast in the role of Greek chorus, comments on the action and the violent, tragic events. Graphic and terrifying though it may be, the story takes on a haunting quality in audio.

Literary Fiction; Western; Thriller.

Robotham, Michael

Shatter. **Joseph O'Loughlin and Victor Ruiz Novels.** Read by Sean Barrett. 2009. Recorded Books. ISBN: 9781436174541. 14.25 hrs. ♟

Psychologist Joe O'Loughlin, who suffers from Parkinson's disease, unsuccessfully tries to stop a woman from jumping off a bridge to her death. This is just the first of a series of maddening cases, and each time, the victim is talking to someone on her cell phone before committing suicide. Who is directing these terrible acts? And why? Barrett reads with an edgy intensity that totally captures this emotionally charged and chilling story. Each characterization, from the sympathetic protagonist to the terrified women and the sinister villain, rings true, as Barrett leads listeners on a roller coaster ride involving insidious and deadly psychological intimidation.

Psychological Suspense; Mystery; Suspense.

More than Meets the Eye:
Edgy, Thoughtful Tales

Sometimes the attraction is more than the story or the setting or the characters: it's the mood projected by the book and enhanced in the audio. Together these elements create thoughtful, sometimes demanding, and disturbing tales that leave us feeling uneasy.

Brockmeier, Kevin

The Brief History of the Dead. Read by Richard Poe. 2006. Recorded Books. ISBN: 1419369091. 8.75 hrs. [Y][A] ▣

Brockmeier explores two worlds in this provocative, haunting novel: the frigid landscape of Antarctica, where scientist Laura Byrd may be the only survivor of a pandemic, and the world of the dead where denizens languish as long as someone on Earth remembers them. Poe's deep voice resonates as he sympathetically presents all characters, living and dead, and navigates the links among story lines, characters, and worlds. His narration moves at a stately pace, intensifying the impact of the evocative imagery and lyrical language in this disturbing, meditative, and imaginative novel.

Literary Fiction.

Manfredo, Lou

Rizzo's War. Read by Bobby Cannavale. 2009. BBC Audiobooks America. ISBN: 9780792766773. 10 hrs.

Cannavale's edgy reading brings a noir feel to the mean streets of Brooklyn, as veteran cop Rizzo breaks in his new partner to the pressures and realities of the job. Smart dialog and richly drawn characters enhance a taut and gritty tale of politics and compromises. Cannavale's Rizzo projects just enough swagger to make him believable both on the job and with his family, and his smoke-darkened voice adds another layer to the characterization, taking us beyond words to the heart of the character.

Mystery.

McEwan, Ian

Saturday. Read by Steven Crossley. 2005. Recorded Books. ISBN: 1419332872. 11 hrs. ♈ 🖘

In this evocative tale focused on language and character, as well as mood, a successful neurosurgeon, Henry Perowne, muses on his life and family, only somewhat disturbed by the home invasion and political protests that threaten his peace. Crossley's performance of the nuanced language and interior perspective reveals Perowne's life in this image-rich stream-of-consciousness, psychologically complex character study. He brings a sense of immediacy to the novel, subtly reflecting changes in mood with tone and cadence shifts in Perowne's interior monologue.

Literary Fiction.

▶ Wilhelm, Kate

The Deepest Water. Read by Marguerite Gavin. 2002. Blackstone Audiobooks. ISBN: 0786193719. 9 hrs.

Gavin's nuanced reading of this psychological tale makes the most of the atmospheric setting in an isolated cabin in the woods of the Pacific Northwest and the haunting, disturbing tone. Abby Conners suspects her novelist father's death may be related to his last unfinished manuscript, and as she begins investigating, she uncovers secrets from his past and clues to his demise—and someone who is willing to kill her to keep these secrets. The sense of foreboding intensifies in this layered tale as painful truths are revealed and the danger grows. The final, chilling twist will both surprise listeners and leave them pondering.

Psychological Suspense.

Winspear, Jacqueline

Maisie Dobbs. **Maisie Dobbs Series.** Read by Rita Barrington. 2005. BBC Audiobooks America. ISBN: 0792734602. 10 hrs. ♈ Ⓨ Ⓐ

Fans appreciate Winspear's haunting mystery series, set in post–World War I London, for many reasons: the complex characters often in desperate circumstances, the provocative issues surrounding the years after the Great War, the compelling stories of war time, and the poignant tone. Listeners feel the full impact of all these elements in Barrington's reading of this first episode, which introduces us to our heroine and vividly explores her life before, during, and after the war. She especially emphasizes the dark tone of this mystery series, filled with haunted, damaged characters, all feeling the lingering effects of their experiences in the war. Lyrical prose and disturbing images add to the bittersweet tale that is more than a mere mystery.

Historical Mystery; Historical Fiction.

Laugh Out Loud Listening:
Humorous Stories

Humor may be universal, but what appeals to one listener may not amuse another. These Humor Sure Bets—tried-and-true titles that work with a variety of listeners—underline the importance of both writing and narrating skill in creating performances that make listeners laugh out loud.

▶ **Buckley, Christopher**
  Florence of Arabia. Read by Carrington MacDuffie. 2004. Books on Tape. ISBN: 9781415905104. 9 hrs.
  MacDuffie shines in this sly send-up of Mideast politics and women's issues, east and west. Buckley's verbal hijinks were made to be heard, and MacDuffie perfectly captures his tongue-in-cheek tone, as the puns roll off her tongue. Florence is a state department official, trying to grant asylum to the prettiest wife of the one of the myriad crown princes of Wasabia. She fails, the princess loses her head, and Florence finds herself undercover in nearby Matar, undercutting government policy with a women's television station. Political satire at its most outrageous, all the better when so artfully rendered in audio format.
  Humor; Thriller.

Grimes, Martha
  Foul Matter. Read by Stephen Hoye. 2003. Books on Tape. ISBN: 0736696555. 12.5 hrs.
  Grimes takes a break from her excellent Richard Jury mystery series to write a book about the publishing world. Take an envious but very wealthy popular writer, add a greedy publisher who will stop at nothing to sign said author, stir in a liberal dose of humor, and you find yourself immersed in a delightfully witty comedy. Our author agrees to sign with a new publisher if the author's perceived nemesis, a literary author, is "removed" from the publisher's list. He probably doesn't expect hit men to be called in. But they are. Hoye's understated reading underlines the innate humor of the situation and characters. Those hapless hit men, reminiscent of the humorous thugs in *Kiss Me, Kate*, steal the show. Forget about the silky prose of Grimes's justifiably famous mysteries and settle in for a few hours of good fun.
  Humor; Caper.

Kinsella, Sophie
  Confessions of a Shopaholic. **Shopaholic Series.** Read by Emily Gray. 2002. Recorded Books. ISBN: 1419304828. 11.75 hrs.
  Whether one cringes at or is delighted by hapless Rebecca Bloomwood's shopping addiction, one can't help but enjoy this masterful performance of her madcap adventures. Gainfully employed—she writes for a financial magazine,

no less—she still cannot manage to stay within her budget, and stiff letters from her bank manager are interspersed throughout the novel, adding to the humorous tone. Gray quickly establishes the chatty, intimate feel of the story and conveys Rebecca's effervescent personality, which ultimately sees her through the tough times.

Humor; Chick Lit; Women's Fiction.

Moore, Christopher

A Dirty Job. Read by Fisher Stevens. 2006. BBC Audiobooks America. ISBN: 9780792739357. 12 hrs. ♉

Moore turns the conventions of the horror genre on its head in this tale featuring madcap humor, a mock epic style starring a hypochondriac hero, and irresistible hell hounds. What's not to like? Charlie Asher, beta male and second-hand shop dealer, becomes a Death Merchant when he confronts Death leaving his dying wife, just after she gave birth to their daughter. Now his job is to collect souls before the forces of evil get them, a task that puts him at odds with those evil forces and leads to even more humor. Stevens makes the most of the multiple plot twists, quirky characters, and great lines. He seems to have had as much fun reading this as listeners will hearing it.

Horror; Humor.

Pratchett, Terry

Going Postal. **Discworld Series.** Read by Stephen Briggs. 2004. HarperAudio. ISBN: 0060740884. 12 hrs.

For elaborate wordplay and jaw-dropping puns, it's hard to do better than Terry Pratchett's mind-boggling Discworld fantasy series. While there's a well-developed fantasy world and series characters that appear throughout, these are books that highlight language, so all are enhanced by excellent narrators like Briggs, who navigates the puns and deadpan humor with aplomb, making even the most ridiculous situations seem realistic. One can start almost anywhere and discover the pleasures of these books. In this, the 30th in the Discworld sequence, swindler Moist van Ludwig can avoid the death penalty if he agrees to revamp the postal system, which he does, with hilarious results.

Fantasy; Humor.

Into the Heart of Darkness: Dangerous Confrontations

Sometimes books feature characters forced to confront deep-seated fears and dangerous opponents. These novels and nonfiction accounts lead listeners into the heart of darkness, physically, emotionally, and spiritually.

▶ Conrad, Joseph

Heart of Darkness. Read by Scott Brick. 2002. Tantor Media. ISBN: 9781400138463. 4.75 hrs. 📖

Although Conrad's classic novel has been frequently recorded, this performance sets the standard. Brick's voice offers just a hint of the British accent, which sets the right tone for Marlowe, an English ship captain, as he relates his tale to fellow passengers on a sea voyage. He tells of his search for a company agent supposedly gone native in the depths of Africa. Brick's performance accentuates the tone. His matter-of-fact reporting of strange events, which become stranger and stranger as the story goes on, leads to a growing realization that madness abounds and that we may all be susceptible to its powerful lure. Mesmerizing and unsettling.

Literary Fiction; Classic.

King, Stephen

The Girl Who Loved Tom Gordon. Read by Anne Heche. 1999. Recorded Books. ISBN: 0788751530. 6.5 hrs. [Y][A]

Nine-year-old Trisha McFarland is walking in the Maine woods with her mother and brother, and as they argue, she steps off the path . . . and is lost. Her phenomenal journey, made only with the meager contents of her day pack, takes her deeper and deeper into the woods, where she is trailed by a beast, a bear who takes on supernatural proportions. With only her Walkman to listen to the Boston Red Sox games and follow her hero, ace relief pitcher Tom Gordon, she confronts her worst fears—and survives. Heche captures her young voice and indomitable spirit in this haunting, psychological tale from the master of horror.

Horror; Coming-of-Age.

Mason, Daniel

The Piano Tuner. Read by Richard Matthews. 2002. Books on Tape. ISBN: 0736688420. 12 hrs. ♛ ☙

London's finest piano tuner Edgar Drake is sent to Burma in 1886 to tune a French grand piano owned by a native warlord. Music to soothe the savage breast, or, in this case, a bellicose prince. Matthews inhabits the complex Drake on his journey, both physical and emotional, as he moves from the safety of London's Victorian mores to another, very different world and culture. Lyrical language, a lush landscape, and dangerous images drive this atmospheric novel and underline the uneasy mood, as protagonist Drake journeys into the jungle of his soul.

Literary Fiction; Historical Fiction.

Millard, Candice

The River of Doubt: Theodore Roosevelt's Darkest Journey. Read by Paul Michael. 2005. Books on Tape. ISBN: 1415924562. 12.25 hrs. Nonfiction.

Having lost his bid for the White House in 1912, Theodore Roosevelt, accompanied by son Kermit, sought solace in adventure and joined a trip to explore the Amazon. No stranger to physical danger, Roosevelt almost met his match in the treacherous terrain filled with deadly fauna, cannibalistic natives, and disease. Michael deftly reflects the strong sense of foreboding that initiates and flows through this tale of adventure and wilderness survival. He portrays Roosevelt, Kermit, a famous Brazilian explorer, and others with minimal accents but acute emotional identification. Roosevelt emerged, having lost a quarter of his body weight, ready for the next challenge. The audio version of this harrowing yet inspirational story draws us into the characters' adventures and makes the rigors of their journey all the more terrifying.

History; Biography.

Penny, Louise

The Brutal Telling. **Inspector Armand Gamache Mysteries.** Read by Ralph Cosham. 2009. Blackstone Audio. ISBN: 9781433297090. 13.5 hrs. ♛

Guided by Inspector Armand Gamache of the Sûreté du Quebec, listeners follow the investigation into the murder of a hermit, which leads us on a harrowing psychological journey deep into the heart of darkness. Gamache and his team follow clues and emotions to discover the terrible truth of the crime and its implications in this 21st-century morality play, which explores the unexpectedly familiar face of evil. Series narrator Cosham embodies the intuitive, intelligent inspector and captures the brooding tone as the investigation leads to someone in the village, a friend whose dark secrets may be too terrible to contemplate. A thoughtful, layered mystery, rich in characters, clues, and poetry.

Mystery.

On the Edge of Your Chair: Suspenseful Tales

Just as their book versions do, many audiobooks keep us on the edge of our chairs, waiting to see what will happen next. Will the hero survive? Will the mission be completed? Narrators employ all their skills to convey story and character, but what they do best is establish the mood and the pace, drawing us into stories and not letting up.

Finder, Joseph

Vanished. **Nick Heller Series.** Read by Holter Graham. 2009. BBC Audiobooks America. ISBN: 9780792765486. 10.5 hrs.

With his mother injured and in the hospital and his father vanished without a trace, young Gabe calls his uncle Nick Heller, an ex–Special Forces solider, and just the man to turn to when there's trouble. As Nick threads his way through multiple scams, layers of secrets, and surprising twists in the labyrinthine plot, Graham's narration keeps the tension building to the final denouement. His expert performance highlights the smart dialog and keeps listeners riveted with the breakneck pace. Audiobooks like this make long car trips a pleasure.

Thriller.

Frost, Mark
The Second Objective. Read by Erik Steele. 2007. Sound Library/BBC Audiobooks America. ISBN: 9780792748434. 10.5 hrs. 🏆

A commando mission, a last ditch effort by the Nazis, places 2,000 German soldiers posing as Americans behind the lines just before the Battle of the Bulge. Their objective is to infiltrate the Allied forces. But a select second group has another objective: to assassinate Eisenhower. It doesn't matter that we know the outcome, Steele's impassioned reading pulls listeners into this claustrophobic "what if" tale, following American and German soldiers alike. Historical details fill the novel, but it is the suspense, building in intensity, that keeps us mesmerized.

Thriller; Historical Fiction; Military Fiction.

▶ **Koontz, Dean R.**
Velocity. Read by Michael Hayden. 2005. Books on Tape. ISBN: 1415921334. 9.5 hrs. [Y][A]

This relentlessly paced novel pits bartender and novelist Billy Wiles against an unknown monster who forces him to make impossible life-and-death decisions time and time again. It starts with a note on his car's windshield, forcing Billy to choose a serial killer's next victim—and escalates into a nightmare situation from which there seems no escape. Hayden first portrays Billy as a rather gullible and confused victim, but later he leads listeners to wonder whether something in Billy's past has put him in jeopardy. Hayden masterfully creates a claustrophobic mood that doesn't let up.

Thriller; Psychological Suspense.

Parker, T. Jefferson
Storm Runners. Read by Christopher Lane. 2007. Brilliance Audio. ISBN: 9781423305873. 9 hrs.

The terrible sense of foreboding hits readers from the very first line of this edgy novel of suspense and never lets up. Ex-cop Matt Stromsoe lost his wife and son in an explosion meant for him. Damaged physically, mentally, and emotionally, he takes a job protecting a popular TV weather woman from a stalker. With that, he becomes involved in a fascinating tale of Southern California's water politics and the science of changing weather. As he protects the quirky weather woman, he also tracks the guy who destroyed his life. Lane's understated reading lets the story speak for itself. He keeps us on edge and builds the tension as the twisted plot lines spin out in this brooding tale of revenge.

Suspense; Weather.

Reich, Christopher
Rules of Deception. **Jonathan Ransom Series.** Read by Paul Michael. 2008. Books on Tape. ISBN: 9781415948309. 14.25 hrs.

This first in Reich's series chronicling the exploits of Jonathan Ransom, a mild-mannered physician who works with Doctors without Borders, introduces the characters and the nightmare that explodes Ransom's perfect world. When his wife is lost in a climbing accident in Switzerland, he discovers she led a secret life as a spy. Thus is he thrown into the world of espionage, fighting for his own life and always wondering whom he can trust. Fast action, a claustrophobic mood, smart dialog, engaging characters, and a wealth of plot twists provide fodder for Michael's narrating skills. His interpretation of the very believable good-guy Ransom resonates, and he adds an edgy intensity to this adrenaline-fueled thriller.

Thriller; Adventure.

A Ghost for Every Listener: Modern Gothic Tales

Gothic elements—mysterious, ghostly happenings—are cropping up in recent novels with such frequency that fans might think we're in the midst of a gothic revival! Audiobooks make these haunting, atmospheric stories even more disquieting, as skillful narrators convey the disturbing sense of unease and the moody tone that are the signature of this style.

Egan, Jennifer

The Keep. Read by Jeff Gurner and Geneva Carr. 2006. BBC Audiobooks America. ISBN: 9780792742616. 8 hrs.

Complete with an ancient castle and a ghost, the sine qua non of the traditional gothic style, this compelling, layered story-within-a-story features estranged cousins, together again after years apart following a teenage prank. Now multimillionaire Howard seems to be offering ne'er-do-well Danny the break—and escape—he needs. Or is this merely elaborate payback? Or could it be that the entire story, including Danny and Howard, is simply the product of a convict's imagination in a prison writing class? Gurner's pitch-perfect narration, interspersed with Carr's account of the writing class, drives this continually unsettling novel in which the heightened atmosphere sets the tone.

Psychological Suspense.

Goodman, Carol

The Drowning Tree. Read by Christine Marshall. 2004. BBC Audiobooks America. ISBN: 079273291X. 13.5 hrs.

All Goodman's novels express a full measure of the gothic, with isolated settings, mysterious events, and lyrical, evocative language to describe enigmatic characters and menacing landscapes. Here, a distinguished alumna presents a controversial lecture at a prestigious private school—and is found dead the next day. A suicide? Her friend Juno, a teacher at the school, doesn't think so, and Juno's investigation into the death of her friend puts her own life in danger. Marshall's narration evokes the intrigue and suspense that underlie the novel. Parallel stories, past and present, and pervasive water images and dreams also add to the distinctly disturbing mood Marshall conveys.

Psychological Suspense; Thriller.

Phillips, Arthur

The Egyptologist. Read by Gianfranco Negroponte, Simon Prebble, Gerard Doyle, and Bianca Amato. 2004. Recorded Books. ISBN: 1402596197. 16.5 hrs.

Phillips plays with gothic trappings in this decidedly creepy, camp novel. There are two requisite castles: the tomb of an apocryphal pharaoh Atumhadu and the Boston townhouse of the wealthy fiancée of hapless archaeologist Ralph Trilipush. There is also a wealth of supernatural happenings and dangers. Told in letters and journal entries provided by a series of unreliable narrators, the complex story focuses predominantly on Trilipush's excavations and descent into insanity. Prebble's portrayal of the disturbed and disturbing archaeologist sets the tone, and supporting characters, including the Australian private investigator who is always just a step behind Trilipush, add to the complex mix of murderous insanity and atmospheric excesses.

Psychological Suspense; Literary Fiction.

▶ **Setterfield, Diane**

The Thirteenth Tale. Read by Bianca Amato and Jill Tanner. 2006. Recorded Books. ISBN: 1428115676. 16 hrs. ⛎ 🏆 Ⓨ Ⓐ 🐚

In a tale rife with supernatural elements and set on England's isolated moors, popular but reclusive author Vida Winter commands Margaret Lea to write her biography. Vida proves an untrustworthy narrator of her own life, but Margaret's explorations into Vida's past, as well as her discoveries about Vida's personal history, lead to dramatic and surprising parallel stories of family secrets and ghostly happenings in this haunting, twisted tale. Narrators Amato, as the naive Margaret, and Tanner, as the elusive Vida, portray their characters to perfection, emphasizing the language and mood that drive this evocative novel.

Literary Fiction; Psychological Suspense.

Simmons, Dan

The Terror. Read by John Lee. 2006. Books on Tape. ISBN: 9781415937136. 28.5 hrs. 🏆

This versatile author, known especially for his science fiction and horror novels, combines historical adventure with gothic style to create a singularly disturbing story. Ostensibly speculating on the fate of the 1845 Franklin expedition's attempt to discover a northwest passage, this story explores the effect of mysterious events, a stalking by an unknown beast, and an uncertain future on a claustrophobic crew of survivors. John Lee's splendid narration captures the growing terror among the men, as well as the overall despair that ultimately destroys them. No isolated, haunted castle here but a lone ship frozen in an unfamiliar environment, in which every threat from within and without is magnified by the unsettled atmosphere.

Literary Fiction; Historical Fiction; Psychological Suspense.

Love and Laughter: Romantic Comedy

Witty repartee, quirky characters, lively dialog, humorous situations, and a heartwarming love story are all vital elements in romantic comedy. The best narrators of romantic comedies place listeners firmly in the story, by participating in the verbal sparring and taking pleasure in the satisfying romance.

Cabot, Meg

Queen of Babble. **Queen of Babble Series.** Read by Justine Eyre. 2006. Books on Tape. ISBN: 9781415932377. 9 hrs.

Naive Lizzie Nichols has almost graduated—there's that annoying little problem of a thesis remaining—but she's determined to finish it up as she jets off to London to join her boyfriend, a guy she's known for one night but corresponded with for months. Needless to say, all does not go as planned, but the chatterbox lands on her feet at a chateau in France and in hot water (as usual) for speaking before thinking. Narrator Eyre clearly relishes the romantic mayhem, as is evidenced in her exuberant reading of this playful tale. An irresistible confection for fans of romantic chick lit and lighthearted love stories.

Romance; Chick Lit; Women's Fiction.

Heyer, Georgette

The Talisman Ring. Read by Phyllida Nash. 2000. BBC Audiobooks/Chivers. ISBN: 9781405672252. 9.5 hrs.

Nash's irresistible pleasure in Heyer's inimitable Georgian-era romp makes this a delight for the ears. With gloriously inane palaver, two pairs of lovers reflecting distinctly different moods (one staid, one irrepressibly romantic), a missing ring, and free traders (i.e., smugglers), the novel feels like a Restoration comedy. Nash gives an equally dazzling performance, allowing tone and cadence to portray each individual character and leaving the listener breathless—and wishing for more.

Romance; Humor.

▶ Phillips, Susan Elizabeth

Natural Born Charmer. **Chicago Stars Series.** Read by Anna Fields. 2007. Books on Tape. ISBN: 9781415937471. 12 hrs. ♟ ♛

This splendid romp introduces football star Dan Robillard to itinerant artist Blue Bailey as she stomps down a deserted road in a beaver suit. Phillips's charming and warmhearted romances offer so many rewards: intriguing characters, unlikely relationships, and sizzling sexual tension, but her deft hand at dialog is what keeps listeners coming back for more. Here the rich banter sets up the lively romance and leads to a satisfying resolution. Fields provides a brilliant interpretation of the novel, catching every nuance of tone and voice. Her rich, husky alto works perfectly for the large cast of characters, from a crotchety old crone to Dan's young half-sister, and she excels in portraying the romantic leads. As the consummate professional, Fields even sought out and included the original music, written by Phillips's son, that forms the backdrop of the story.

Romance; Humor.

Quinn, Julia

What Happens in London. Read by Rosalyn Landor. 2009. Books on Tape. ISBN: 9780307578327. 10 hrs. ♛

Quinn's humor lies principally in character and language but it's also physical, and all are enhanced in Landor's exuberant reading. Lady Olivia Bevelstoke, a bluestocking who prefers facts (she's a newspaper reader) to fiction (she abhors novels) is bored. Until the enigmatic Sir Harry Valentine, rumored to have killed his fiancée, moves next door. When Harry catches her spying on him, he embarks upon windowsill conversations that lead to real affection and love. Landor's skill at rendering their verbal sparring and Quinn's witty dialog is first-rate; you can hear their affection and growing pleasure in each other in her voice. A charming romance with a touch of melodrama, a dash of danger, and a good deal of laugh out loud humor.

Historical Romance; Humor.

Willig, Lauren

The Secret History of the Pink Carnation. **Pink Carnation Series.** Read by Kate Reading. 2005. Books on Tape. ISBN: 1415916926. 13.25 hrs.

Take one spunky Harvard Ph.D. candidate researching English spies during the French Revolution; add a stiff-upper-lip Englishman whose family papers hold secrets to the identities of several spies; mix in the historical tale of the said spies and their humorous and dangerous escapades; and leaven with a large measure of wit. The result is a romp filled with swashbuckling adventure and multiple romances, not to mention extravagant costumes and flamboyant wit. Willig alternates historical and contemporary tales, provides parallel romantic entanglements, and offers fascinating historical details. Reading's accomplished narration keeps characters and time periods straight, and her performance reflects her own obvious pleasure in the adventures.

Historical Romance; Humor.

Chapter Three

Story

Readers and listeners alike recognize the pleasures of a good story well told. In audio, the listening experience allows us to sink more deeply into stories, transported by the narrators' voices as they draw us ever further into the tale. As with all audio versions, the narrator's voice shapes the story and skillfully conveys the author's intention through such vocal manipulations as a rapid acceleration of pace, a subtle pause to allow a point to reach home, or the deft delivery of witty banter. As a result, in the best audio editions, the narration and narrator enhance the story. In fact, sometimes the story is easier to follow when listening, because we can't skim over passages when the pacing increases. We hear every detail and follow the story to the end. Whether the plot follows a quest or chronicles a disaster, reflects today's headlines or tells a classic tale, stories provide the stage for narrator performances as they guide us through the action.

Lasting Pleasures: Classics Come Alive

Although students often rely on audiobooks to "slog through" the classics for assignments, many others are discovering the pleasures of listening to skilled narrators interpret titles they've read before—or may never have had time to read. With classics there is always the pleasure of discovery, whether in reading a classic for the first time or in rereading. Audio versions allow new insights; a narrator's inflection opens new avenues to explore and adds to the layers of meaning and appreciation. Among the best of the best are the following.

Beowulf. Translated by Seamus Heaney. Read by George Guidall. 2004. Recorded Books. ISBN: 9781402581816. 4.25 hrs. Y A

Performing Heaney's fresh and vital translation, Guidall reflects the stately cadences and majesty of this timeless classic—the author of which is unknown—a tale of fifth-century Scandinavia and the mighty warrior who killed monsters and governed wisely until he met his fate in a battle with a dragon in its lair. Guidall's elegant reading invigorates this excellent modern translation and makes the hero in all his dignity accessible to a modern audience.

Literary Fiction; Classic.

▶ Homer

The Iliad. Translated and read by Stanley Lombardo. 2007. Parmenides Audio. ISBN: 1930972083. 17 hrs.

Lombardo's fresh translation of this classic story of the Trojan War, which he reads with confidence and élan, shimmers with energy and new life. Colloquial jargon and modern language update this epic tale for modern ears without sacrificing familiar metaphors and images. As a classicist, Lombardo understands the poem's roots in the oral tradition, and his translation and performance emphasize the rhythms and cadence that transform speech into poetry in this timeless tale of adventure, revenge, and one man's anger and its consequences.

Literary Fiction; Classic; Adventure.

James, Henry

The Turn of the Screw. Read by Simon Vance and Vanessa Benjamin. 2009. Blackstone. ISBN: 9781433274084. 5 hrs. Y A

Although Vance sets up this classic ghost story told on a Christmas Eve around the fire after dinner, Benjamin recreates the characters, giving voice to the unnamed governess and her two young charges. Life seems normal enough, as the new governess takes over her duties, until she starts seeing people whom no one else sees. Benjamin's tone changes from sweet and matter-of-fact to edgy intensity verging on hysteria as the tension and sense of menace build in this moody and atmospheric tale of children held in thrall to their former governess and houseman.

Classic; Literary Fiction; Horror.

Lee, Harper

To Kill a Mockingbird. Read by Sissy Spacek. 2006. Recorded Books. ISBN: 1428113517. 12 hrs. 👤 🏆 Y A 📖

Fans of the movie version starring Gregory Peck as lawyer and father Atticus Finch may have forgotten that the novel is told through the eyes of young Scout Finch. Spacek's heartfelt performance captures the young girl's point of view and reveals events and relationships through her eyes. Listeners are transported back to the quiet Alabama town, where the gossipy, drowsy daily life has been disrupted by violence.

Literary Fiction; Classic; Coming-of-Age.

Stevenson, Robert Louis
  Treasure Island. Read by Alfred Molina. 2007. Listening Library. ISBN: 9780739350461. 7 hrs. 🏅
    Join young Jim Hawkins in search of treasure with quintessential pirate Long John Silver and his perfidious mates. Molina's exuberant performance, complete with a wide range of accents to fit each character and station, makes listeners a party to the adventures. The sea shanties that introduce each disk add to the flavor and the pleasure of the tale. A classic for all ages.
    Classic; Adventure; Family Listening.

Adrenaline Redux: Classic Thrillers

Audio is one of the best ways to appreciate the classics in any genre, whether for "rereading" or as an introduction to a classic work. Several of these thrillers have benefited from new recordings by narrators who excel at allowing stories to shine.

Fleming, Ian
  From Russia with Love. **James Bond Series.** Read by Simon Vance (as Robert Whitfield). 2000. Blackstone Audiobooks. ISBN: 078619829X. 9 hrs.
    Most of us know James Bond from the movies where cartoon plots and characters are played to the hilt. The books are different; for example, here Bond lacks the elaborate weapons that play such important roles in the films. In fact, we don't even meet Bond until midway through this book, when he is set up to fall in love with a beautiful Russian spy and meet his end on the famed Orient Express. Who could ask for more? Vance does it all—the urbane British accent that personifies this most sophisticated of spies, the multiple accents and foreign phrases of the other players, and the dramatic final encounter with the viperous Rosa Kleb.
    Thriller; Classic.

Follett, Ken
  Eye of the Needle. Read by Eric Lincoln, Roslyn Alexander, Richard Lavin, Patricia Pickering, Robert Hunt, R. William Mueller, Derrell Capes, and Bradley Mott. 2007. Brilliance Audio. ISBN: 9781423328612. 9 hrs. 🏆
    This classic World War II espionage thriller pits German agent Der Nadel (the Needle) against British Intelligence in a race to keep the news of the D-day invasion site from Hitler. Lincoln provides the background narration, while the cast voices the dialog to create very human characters with spot-on accents, inflection, and cadence. We're pulled into the spy's consciousness to the extent that we almost find ourselves in sympathy with him. In the end, the unlikeliest character saves the day, aided by a terrific storm and the dangerous terrain of the Scottish coast. Heart-stopping tension, very human characters, deadly

drama, and a dangerous landscape add up to a breathtaking adventure. The new recording speaks to the staying power of this thriller.

Thriller; Historical Fiction; Classic.

▶ **Forsyth, Frederic**
The Day of the Jackal. Read by Simon Prebble. 2009. Blackstone Audiobooks. ISBN: 9781441711625. 13 hrs. ♛

Step-by-agonizing-step, Prebble leads listeners through the elaborate preparations by the Jackal, an anonymous English assassin, who has been hired to kill Charles DeGaulle shortly after the French withdraw from Algeria. As each detail falls into place, tension builds, and the Jackal's success seems assured, and it would be, except for the unexceptional French policeman who was assigned to the case after a tip that the hit had been planned. Faithfully rendered characters, from the cold and affectless assassin to the earnest policeman; authentic historical details; and the perfectly orchestrated cat-and-mouse pursuit make this book a classic. Prebble's skilled reading makes it unforgettable.

Thriller; Suspense; Classic.

LeCarré, John
The Spy Who Came In from the Cold. **George Smiley Series.** Read by Frank Muller. 1987. Recorded Books. ISBN: 9781419321283. 6.5 hrs. ♛

Muller's haunting narration of this classic tale still resonates with listeners. In typical LeCarré fashion, the tale is dark and dramatic. A menacing atmosphere pervades, underscored by Muller's edgy reading, as British spy Alec Leamas, stranded in East Germany during the Cold War, slowly realizes that he has been played in an elaborate plot, tricked by guys bad and good, for in LeCarré's world betrayal is as likely from within as without. Positively chilling.

Thriller; Literary Fiction; Classic.

Ludlum, Robert
The Bourne Identity. **Jason Bourne Series.** Read by Scott Brick. 2008. Books on Tape. ISBN: 9781415961308. 22.25 hrs.

This classic espionage series has been revitalized by excellent movie adaptations, but the original stories remain hard to resist. In this first of the series, Jason Bourne suffers a severe head injury that gives him amnesia, and only when he must run for his life does he begin to uncover who he is and what he was doing when everything went black. Nonstop action and plot twists in almost every chapter keep us glued to our earphones, as we listen to discover what will happen next. Brick never hesitates as he delivers the adrenaline-paced dialog with verve. He skillfully channels the character of the amnesiac assassin and conveys the shock of each revelation as Bourne slowly realizes who and what he is. Brick's narration leaves listeners breathless.

Thriller; Adventure; Classic.

Oh No! Disaster Stories

Disasters come in all shapes and sizes from diverse causes, and their impact may be wide-ranging or limited in scope. Reports of disasters can be compelling and moving in both fiction and nonfiction, and in both cases skilled narrators make these stories personal and horrifying, no matter the scale of the devastation.

Brooks, Geraldine
Year of Wonders. Read by Josephine Bailey. 2001. Books on Tape. ISBN: 0736675574. 10.5 hrs. Y A ♨
> The discovery of plague in a community has always been an ominous portent of disaster. Here Bailey dramatically recounts the story of a 17th-century English village that, having been infected with the plague, cuts itself off to stop the spread of the contagion. This intimate, first-person account captures the frustration, fear, and resignation of the villagers and intensifies listeners' sympathy. Bailey's reading highlights the lyrical prose as well as the strong sense of foreboding. All cannot end well in this elegant, thoughtful, haunting tale.
> Historical Fiction; Disaster; Medical Disaster.

Harris, Robert
Pompeii. Read by John Lee. 2003. Books on Tape. ISBN: 0736695982. 10.5 hrs. Y A ♨
> It is 79 C.E. and a water engineer is called to the slopes of Mount Vesuvius to diagnose a blockage in the aqueduct. He discovers the problem—and much more. Strange occurrences on the mountain leave him puzzled and uneasy. Listeners know, of course, that Vesuvius is poised to erupt, but life goes on until the inevitable happens. Contributing to the sense of menace, Lee's deep, sonorous voice sets the tone for this novel from the very beginning. Rich in historical, cultural, and social details, as well vulcanology, this intelligent take on a historical catastrophe should please listeners on many levels.
> Historical Fiction; Disaster.

▶ **McCullough, David**
The Johnstown Flood. Read by Edward Herrmann. 2005. Simon & Schuster. ISBN: 0743540867. 10 hrs. Nonfiction.
> Herrmann's mellow voice enlivens McCullough's riveting nonfiction account of the 1889 disaster: an earth dam holding back a mountain resort lake has been weakened by rains and fails, flooding the central Pennsylvania town of Johnstown, killing more than 2,000 people. Of course there's political chicanery involving the great industrialists of the age, whose negligence created a national scandal. McCullough's scrupulous research and interviews with survivors of the disaster forge a fascinating picture of the people and the times.

Herrmann's deft narration transports listeners back to this so-called Gilded Age and catapults us into the midst of the disaster.
History; Disaster.

Preston, Richard
The Hot Zone. Read by Richard M. Davidson. 1995. Recorded Books. ISBN: 9781402553721. 11 hrs. Nonfiction.

This is the granddaddy of medical disaster books, spawner of dozens of novels and nonfiction titles alerting the world to the terrible potential of deadly viruses lurking in the environment. In this nonfiction offering, the Ebola virus is mistakenly released from a Virginia research facility. With journalistic equanimity (and just a hint of terror) Davidson relates the history of the virus from its emergence in Africa to the steps taken to contain an outbreak in the United States, along with the graphic details of the disease. His voice reflects the building tension and the nightmare mood of this compelling account, all the more frightening because it is true. His authoritative reading reminds us that a similar disaster could happen again.
Disaster; Medical Disaster.

Winchester, Simon
Krakatoa: The Day the World Exploded, August 27, 1883. Read by Simon Winchester. 2003. HarperCollins. ISBN: 0060530677. 12 hrs. Nonfiction.

What a story! This is a minutely detailed tale of a disaster—the eruption of Krakatoa in Indonesia—along with a fascinating exploration of its impact on other natural systems (including a tsunami that killed thousands, followed by years of weather disruption), as well as its long reaching social, cultural, and political effects. But it also includes a history of plate tectonics (which explains the cause of the eruption) and telegraphy, the means by which the news circled the globe. Author/narrator Winchester shares his expertise and enthusiasm as he conveys both the drama and the scientific implications of events. He takes listeners with him to the spot and unfurls his fascinating tale with passion and assurance, proving his skill as a storyteller in print and in audio.
Disaster.

Suspenseful Mixology: Genre Blends

Fans of genre fiction know that some titles refuse to fit nicely within genre boxes. These edgy tales blend suspense, an element of mystery, and often a psychological twist to produce chills and thrill fans with their interesting characters and stories.

Child, Lee
One Shot. **Jack Reacher Series.** Read by Dick Hill. 2005. Brilliance. ISBN: 9781593555191. 12 hrs.

Jack Reacher is a loner, a paladin who travels light—he buys inexpensive clothes and throws them away—and seldom shares his thoughts or his jobs. He is attracted to trouble, which is a good thing since he is amazingly adept as a fixer. In this ninth book in the series, he is called to Indiana by a man accused of being a sniper who murdered five people. Reacher has reason to hate this man, yet he comes with all his ex-military police skills to find the real killer. Hill has narrated the entire series, and his portrayal of the laconic Reacher is spot-on, low key until the action and suspense become so intense that we can barely stand to listen. A memorable story and performance. This is a great series for long car trips.

Thriller; Mystery; Suspense.

Hart, Erin
Haunted Ground. **Nora Gavin and Cormac Maguire Series.** Read by Jennifer McMahon. 2003. Books on Tape. ISBN: 0736693254. 13.5 hrs. 🏆

When peat cutters in rural Ireland turn up a severed head, an Irish archaeologist and American pathologist are called in to investigate. Villagers wonder if the bodies of a landowner's recently missing wife and son will also emerge from the bog. The lyrical prose lends itself to audio, and McMahon makes the most of atmosphere and the psychological undercurrents that give the story an almost gothic feel. Her grasp of accents—Gaelic, English, American, and Indian—add to the effect, as listeners are drawn into this richly detailed story, framed by music and folktales. Chilling and intensely suspenseful, this is a treat for the ears and the intellect.

Mystery; Suspense; Psychological Suspense.

▶ **Iles, Greg**
Turning Angel. **Penn Cage Series.** Read by Dick Hill. 2005. Brilliance. ISBN: 9781590866061. 16 hrs.

Few thrillers are as evocative of time and place as the Penn Cage series by Iles. Natchez, Mississippi, is on its way down, and the brooding sense of despair in the town permeates these already dark plots, adding a bleak melancholy to the dripping Southern heat and humidity. Penn returns home to Natchez to find his best friend accused of murdering the high school senior with whom he was having an affair. Hill's smooth Southern accent draws listeners into Penn's first-person tale. He also brings a large supporting cast to life, including the black and white Southerners who populate Natchez and a Bosnian student who just happens to be a drug dealer. Natchez itself becomes a character as well, from the underbelly of corruption to the dreams of some of its citizens.

Suspense; Mystery; Thriller.

King, Laurie R.
Keeping Watch. Read by Richard Ferrone. 2003. Recorded Books. ISBN: 1402542275. 16.25 hrs.

Although best known for her mystery series reviving Sherlock Holmes, King has also written provocative titles of mystery and gripping psychological suspense. Allen Carmichael, an emotionally damaged Vietnam vet, helps abused children and women escape their tormenters. His last case, rescuing a 12-year-old boy from his abusive father, may have been a mistake. Something nags at his mind, and when he investigates further into the boy's life, he discovers the terrible consequences of his act. Ferrone's dark and gravelly voice reflects the dangerous themes, including Allen's flashbacks to his wartime experiences. He navigates layer upon layer of story and character, exposing deadly mind games and potential dangers. Ferrone carefully builds the intensity of this emotional story in which nothing is quite what it seems and leads readers to the devastating conclusion. A breathtaking performance of a disturbing tale.

Psychological Suspense; Mystery.

McDermid, Val

The Torment of Others. **Tony Hill and Carol Jordan Series.** Read by Gerard Doyle. 2005. Recorded Books. ISBN: 1419333771. 14.5 hrs.

Scottish police detective Carol Jordan, a by-the-book cop, turns to psychologist, and sometimes-colleague, Tony Hill for help with a baffling case. Prostitutes are being horrifically murdered, exactly as they were in a former case, but the killer from that case is locked in a mental institution. Is it a copycat or, as Hill believes, is the incarcerated murderer somehow directing the action? What makes the narration so difficult is that Doyle must voice not only the large cast of characters but also the inner voices of Jordan and Hill. That he succeeds so well is testimony to his skill at embodying fascinating characters working out their personal demons amidst a body-littered landscape. Like the others in the Jordan/Hill series, this fourth entry presents the dark side of humanity through elegant prose, a complex and layered story line, and intriguing characters.

Suspense; Mystery; Psychological Suspense.

Golden Oldies: Classic Mysteries

These titles from the Golden Age of the mystery genre remind listeners of the pleasures of listening to classic tales well read. Not all the really good stuff was published in the last decade!

Christie, Agatha

Death on the Nile. **Hercule Poirot Series.** Read by David Suchet. 2005. Audio Partners. ISBN: 1572704756. 8.5 hrs.

Even on vacation drifting up the Nile, Hercule Poirot finds a murder to investigate. A beautiful American woman is killed and her husband suffers a bullet wound in the leg. It's no surprise that all the travelers seem to have a motive for the murder, or the opportunity, or both! This mystery offers the best of the Golden Age tradition with multiple clues and red herrings, hidden secrets, and a sleuth who proves more agile than the murderer. Narrator Suchet portrayed Poirot on the PBS *Mystery!* series, and his Belgian-accented detective exudes charm. Suchet hits all the right notes as he creates accents for the large, diverse cast, reflecting changes in tone with each action and revelation. He masterfully spools out Christie's devilishly clever plot and pulls listeners along as Poirot untangles the web of secrets and jealousy.

Mystery; Classic.

McBain, Ed

Kiss: A Novel of the 87th Precinct. **87th Precinct Mysteries.** Read by David Colacci. 2009. Brilliance. MP-3 CD ISBN: 9781423385837. 9 hrs.

With his long-running series of big city police squad mysteries, begun in the mid-1950s and continuing until his death in 2005, McBain set the standard for a new kind of mystery, one that blended multiple cases and characters. *Kiss*, originally published in 1994, demonstrates his skill at presenting complex characters and well-plotted puzzles involving solidly researched police procedures, as well as authentic tone and language. Here, regulars Steve Carella and Meyer Meyer investigate attempts to murder a beautiful blonde, while Steve must also attend the trial of his father's murderer. Colacci's adept reading capitalizes on McBain's skill at characterization and language. Listeners recognize each familiar character, and the dialog, sometimes rapid-fire, sometimes more thoughtful, keeps us entranced. The recording is a tribute to McBain's enduring skill and popularity.

Mystery; Classic.

Sayers, Dorothy L.

Strong Poison. **Lord Peter Wimsey Series.** Read by Ian Carmichael. 2007. BBC Audiobooks America. ISBN: 9781572708587. 7.5 hrs.

Audio mystery fans should be grateful to BBC Audiobooks America for bringing out lovely new editions of Sayers's classic mysteries, set in England in the 1920s and 1930s and starring amateur sleuth Lord Peter Wimsey. Carmichael, who played Wimsey on the PBS *Mystery!* series, has the voices just right—from the proper Lord Peter, whose unusual vulnerability suggests that his interest in Harriet is more than merely legal, to Harriet, whose husky voice suits the no-nonsense mystery writer accused of killing her boyfriend. Secondary characters—especially the very proper Bunter, Wimsey's man, and the ever-efficient Miss Climpson—stand out in this recording. As always, Sayers sets up an intricate puzzle, rich in dark secrets and hidden motives.

Mystery; Classic.

Stout, Rex

A Family Affair. **Nero Wolfe Series.** Read by Michael Prichard. 2005. Audio Partners. ISBN: 1572704942. 5.5 hrs.

When his favorite waiter arrives in the middle of the night seeking Nero Wolfe's help, only to be killed by an explosion in the brownstone's guest room,

Wolfe feels personally involved in this complex puzzle centered on politics. Prichard tells it all from the inimitable Archie Goodwin's perspective, as he provides the legs for the investigation and matches wits with his boss. Although originally published in 1975, Stout's last mystery feels right up to date with Prichard's fresh performance. His sonorous voice highlights the serious aspects of the case as well as Archie's wisecracks.

Mystery; Classic.

▶ **Tey, Josephine**
The Daughter of Time. **Alan Grant Series.** Read by Derek Jacobi. 2002. BBC Audiobooks America. ISBN: 9780792754930. 5.25 hrs.

Confined to a hospital after an accident, Scotland Yard's Inspector Grant is bored, until a friend, aware of Grant's skill at reading faces, brings him a stack of pictures from the National Portrait Gallery. Flummoxed by his reaction to Richard III, whom he sees as a strong and caring leader, he sends his friends out to research Richard's life. Was he wronged by Shakespeare? It's almost impossible to resist Jacobi's animated narration. He moves seamlessly between contemporary and historical stories, adding detail upon detail, and revealing the nature of each character through vocal nuances. Jacobi manages the multiple time lines and characters with charm and aplomb, transforming the investigations into a fascinating historical mystery.

Mystery; Classic.

It's All in the Details—and It's All Details: Microhistories

Microhistories take seemingly inconsequential events and pursue their extensive impact. Fascinating details and quirky topics attract readers and listeners to these tales.

Brookes, Tim
Guitar: An American Life. Read by Tim Brookes. 2005. Blackstone Audiobooks. ISBN: 0786178884. 11.5 hrs. Nonfiction.

Brookes traces the history of the guitar in America back to its roots, probably brought by Spanish explorers, through the modern era. He brings an irresistible enthusiasm to his topic, and his passion illuminates the history. He places the guitar into the framework of American life with excerpts from its history as well as biographies of great musicians, not to mention a personal touch as he watches his own guitar being built. Only excerpts from the musical works discussed would make this recording better.

History; Popular Culture.

Johnson, Steven
Ghost Map: The Story of London's Most Terrifying Epidemic—and How It Changed Science, Cities, and the Modern World. Read by Alan Sklar. 2006. Tantor Media. ISBN: 9781400132980. 8.5 hrs. Nonfiction. 🐚

By mapping the spread of cholera in 19th-century London, Dr. John Snow changed the way we view contagion, as this fascinating microhistory demonstrates. Although the book itself contains illustrations, Sklar's masterful narration provides all the information we need to plot the spread of the disease and learn of its effects on the people and economy of London. His captivating performance of this real-life detective story underlines the authenticity of the account as well as its human side, as he vivifies London and unfolds medical history.

History; Medicine; Popular Science.

▶ **Kurlansky, Mark**
1968: The Year that Rocked the World. Read by Christopher Cazenove. 2004. New Millennium Audio. ISBN: 1590074459. 16.5 hrs. Nonfiction. ♛

As George Carlin said, if you can remember the 1960s, you weren't really there. That may be true, but whether you were actually there or not, this fascinating book will take you back. British actor Cazenove narrates this intimate perspective on a year rich in events in diverse arenas: athletic, political, social, and military. He conveys the distinctive cadence of Kurlansky's prose, and his British accent underlines the international scope of this mesmerizing history. For those who do remember and for those who should.

History; Popular Culture.

Pomerantz, Gary M.
Wilt, 1962: The Night of 100 Points and the Dawn of a New Era. Read by Stephen Hoye. 2005. Books on Tape. ISBN: 141592130X. 10.5 hrs. Nonfiction.

With vivid details this journalistic account documents the March 2, 1962, game in Hershey, Pennsylvania, when "The Big Dipper" Wilt Chamberlain's talent and desire to set a record revolutionized professional basketball and boosted the sport's popularity. The backstory follows Chamberlain's career and the world of professional basketball, while offering insights into a changing era. Hoye's smooth baritone introduces listeners to Chamberlain's magnetic personality and leads us into his world on and off the basketball court. His crisp reporting of characters and events makes listeners feel as if we are there on the night that changed the course of sports history and turned professional basketball into the superstar sport it is today. You don't have to be a fan to appreciate this story and the achievement. An added bonus on the audio is the recording of the fourth quarter of the game. How that recording was discovered is a story all its own.

Sports; Biography.

Winchester, Simon

The Map that Changed the World: William Smith and the Birth of Modern Geology. Read by Simon Winchester. 2001. HarperCollins. ISBN: 0694525219. 10 hrs. Nonfiction.

In this intriguing exploration of the history of earth science, Winchester tracks both William Smith's life and his interest in the fossils he discovered as a canal builder. His research into these fossils led to his conviction that rocks held the secrets of the earth's history. Though not a trained narrator, Winchester reads with passion and the authority of an expert who can make his subject both interesting and understandable to a lay audience.

History; Popular Science.

It's the Law: Legal Thrillers

Legal thrillers and mysteries with strong legal themes offer myriad possibilities for writers—and fans—to enjoy the intricacies of the legal system. Whether you prefer fast-paced action-filled dramas or more measured and provocative character studies, there's something here for every listener.

Connelly, Michael

The Lincoln Lawyer. **Mickey Haller Series.** Read by Adam Grupper. 2005. Books on Tape. ISBN: 1415923299. 10.5 hrs. ♛

Los Angeles lawyer Mickey Haller isn't above playing fast and loose with the law. He defends mostly deadbeats from the back seat of his Lincoln town car, and he's a scrapper of questionable morals. But when he finally must defend an innocent client, both he and listeners are in for some surprises. Grupper's smart young voice convincingly portrays this cynical lawyer with wit and attitude. He makes the most of the snappy dialog and portrays the double-crosses and plot twists with élan in this fast-paced legal thriller. Fans of Connelly's long-running Harry Bosch series will be fascinated as the connections between the two series characters unfold.

Legal Thriller.

Grisham, John

The Firm. Read by Scott Brick. 2002. Books on Tape. ISBN: 0736688609. 16.5 hrs.

Nearly 20 years after the book was published, Grisham's blockbuster legal thriller still delivers with its quick pacing, likeable characters (as well as those we love to hate), provocative story lines, and atmosphere of building suspense that explodes in the denouement. Brick takes listeners inside the characters and their dilemmas and makes us feel the frisson of danger at every turn. This performance of the quintessential David vs. Goliath, page-turning legal thriller about a young lawyer who accepts an offer that may be too good to be true will please even those who have read the book and seen the film.

Legal Thriller.

Scottoline, Lisa

Courting Trouble. **Rosato and Associates Series.** Read by Barbara Rosenblat. 2002. Recorded Books. ISBN: 9781402529672. 11 hrs.

New attorney Ann Murphy has squirreled herself away for a weekend to prepare for a big case, only to open the morning paper and see a headline proclaiming her murder. She came to Philadelphia to escape a stalker, and now she's on the run again, trying to juggle the case and hoping her new partners can help her find the murderer before he realizes she's still alive. Courtroom drama and investigation blend in a fast-paced tale of stalked turned stalker. Series narrator Rosenblat's pitch-perfect characterizations of this large cast add to listeners' pleasure in this series centered on a female law firm in Philadelphia.

Legal Thriller.

▶ Turow, Scott

Reversible Errors. **Kindle County Series.** Read by J. R. Horne. 2002. Books on Tape. ISBN: 0736688811. 13.5 hrs.

Fans of character-centered legal thrillers will find much to appreciate in this complex and provocative story of a corporate lawyer who takes on a pro bono death row appeal. He doubts he'll find anything new in the 10-year-old case, but when another inmate confesses to the crime, the district attorney's tight case begins to unravel. Horne's narration captures the cadence of the terrific dialog and sets the tone for Turow's exploration into the moral and legal questions that arise as he peels away the artifice of case and character. This is about characters as much as the law, and each receives a unique voice through which Horne reveals their fallibility in both their professional and personal lives. A fascinating exploration of the law and those who sometimes make it work.

Legal Thriller.

Wilhelm, Kate

A Wrongful Death. **Barbara Holloway Series.** Read by Carrington MacDuffie. 2007. Blackstone Audiobooks. ISBN: 9781433206382. 9.5 hrs.

Series heroine and lawyer Barbara Holloway turns investigator in this complex, family-centered story involving a mother and son on the run after discovering illegal activities in the family business. Holloway's legal expertise helps her sort out the complex puzzle in this compelling tale that has more action outside than inside the courtroom. Narrator MacDuffie's sensitive reading perfectly reflects the characters and their emotions, from the introspective Holloway, faced with changes in her life, to the young boy in danger. She pulls us into the dramatic story and its sympathetic characters, as we become participants in this complex tale.

Legal Thriller; Mystery.

Layered Tales: Fact and Fiction

Research suggests that every reader reads a different version of every book, with certain elements resonating more than others. These titles offer layers of meaning that enhance the impact of the books and appeal to listeners on multiple levels.

Chevalier, Tracy
The Lady and the Unicorn. Read by Terry Donnelly and Robert Blumenfeld. 2004. BBC Audiobooks America. ISBN: 0792731131. 8 hrs. 🏆 🕮

Chevalier offers fascinating insights into the history of a set of six tapestries, woven during the 15th century in Brussels for a Parisian social climber. Donnelly and Blumenfeld alternate as they relate the stories of the artist who designed the masterpieces, the daughters of the house who inspired him, and the multiple weavers in Brussels, with each story given appropriate accents and vocal variations. Their voices reveal the layers of the novel: an intimate look at the lives of the characters, the creation of a work of art (with fascinating details of the techniques of planning, dying the yarn, and weaving), and a glimpse into the social and historical details of the times. Authentic detail blended with fully imagined lives.

Historical Fiction; Art.

Harris, Robert
The Ghost. Read by Roger Rees. 2007. Recorded Books. ISBN: 9781428169227. 10 hrs. 🏆

When Great Britain's longest-enduring prime minister leaves office and writes his memoir, he employs a ghost writer. His memoir writing is interrupted when the ghost writer, who may have uncovered unwelcome secrets, dies mysteriously. Enter the unnamed protagonist, a second ghost writer, who begins work on the memoir anew. Rees's narration imbues this tangled tale, as dark and wild as the dangerous wintry landscape on Martha's Vineyard where it's set, with a distinct uneasiness, as the second ghost writer also uncovers the ex-prime minister's dark secrets. Listeners will appreciate the ghost conceit, with its several layers: the current ghost writer, the ghost of the first ghost writer, and the ghost of the prime minister's crimes. With his precise reading, Rees enhances the listener's experience of the novel and understanding of the characters. Darkly atmospheric, claustrophobic, and disturbing, this is a truly haunting story.

Literary Fiction; Psychological Suspense.

Nafisi, Azar
Reading Lolita in Tehran: A Memoir in Books. Read by Lisette Lecat. 2004. Recorded Books. ISBN: 9781402592836. 18.5 hrs. Nonfiction. 🏆 🕮

Nafisi's classic examination of life in postrevolutionary Iran combines the best features of memoir, social history, and literary criticism, and Lecat's remarkable reading invites listeners to participate in Nafisi's disturbing yet up-lifting story. On one level, this memoir reveals how Nafisi and her friends sur-vived the changes that led to a more and more oppressive government and how that government affected the standing of her female students and her own abil-ity to teach. On another level, it provides a compelling social history of turbu-lent times. And, finally, it offers vibrant literary criticism, as Nafisi lectures on authors such as Nabokov and Austen. Works written halfway around the world and sometimes centuries before current events still resonate with Nafisi, her students, and with the listeners as we reconsider the value of literature in all times. Lecat's narration is so intimate and compelling that we feel as if we're part of the story and unfolding events.

Memoir; Literary Criticism; Social History.

▶ **Shaffer, Mary Ann, and Annie Barrows**
The Guernsey Literary and Potato Peel Pie Society. Read by Paul Boehmer, Susan Duerden, Rosalyn Landor, John Lee, and Juliet Mills. 2008. Books on Tape. ISBN: 9781415954409. 8 hrs.

This colorful epistolary novel sports multiple narrators as well as a layered story of characters, history, and the power of books. Journalist Juliet Ashton, who wrote a lively column during World War II, finds herself at loose ends af-ter the war and seeks another assignment. That project unfolds when she begins a correspondence with Dawsey Adams. He and his Guernsey Island friends write of events on Guernsey during the war when it was occupied by the Nazis. Like the best historical fiction, this centers on history made personal through the experiences of those who lived it. Books played an important role, as the islanders formed the eponymous book club, and the value of books in seeing one through tough times stands out as the inspirational message of this tale. This story is made for audio with each member of the full cast recording voicing a particular character, revealing personality and literary tastes with accents and inflections. By turns heartwarming and humorous, tragic and upbeat, inspira-tional and matter of fact, these performances offer listeners a glimpse into lives in perilous times.

Gentle Reads; Historical Fiction.

Shreve, Anita
A Wedding in December. Read by Linda Emond. 2005. Books on Tape. ISBN: 9781415925782. 10 hrs.

Images of 9/11 as well as the Halifax Explosion of 1917 are woven through this story of friendship, choices, and consequences. Friends from an exclusive prep school reunite 27 years later for a wedding. Parallel story lines (the disas-ters of 2001 and 1917) and characters (a friend lost to suicide in their youth and the bride dying of cancer in the present) drive this graceful novel of lost love and hidden truths. Emond holds listeners with her exceptional reading, distinguishing among the large cast by pitch and tone, as she carefully reflects the subtle nuances of meaning. Her narration sets us clearly in each time period, past and present, revealing the interwoven themes. A compelling yet bittersweet character study.

Literary Fiction; Women's Fiction.

Other Voices: Multicultural Experiences

Immigrants add their distinctive voices to the American experience, and accents add to our appreciation of their languages, while hearing often makes foreign-seeming words and phrases much easier to understand. The literary style of these books also makes them good suggestions for fans of literary fiction.

Díaz, Junot

The Brief Wondrous Life of Oscar Wao. Read by Jonathan Davis and Staci Snell. 2007. Books on Tape. ISBN: 9781415941942. 16 hrs. ♈ ⓎⒶ ☙

Although complicated with multiple layers and retellings of stories by different characters, Díaz's semiautobiographical novel, rich in slang and lyrical language, is meant to be heard. Davis excels at interpreting the male characters in New Jersey and the Dominican Republic, and his confiding voice with its light Dominican accent draws us into the engaging, energetic, flamboyant tale. Snell performs the women's roles with less élan, but together they create an exceptional audio experience that explores the influences from both the Dominican Republic and the United States that contribute to the making of this nerdy misfit hero.

Literary Fiction; Family Saga; Multicultural Fiction.

Erdrich, Louise

The Plague of Doves. Read by Peter Francis James and Kathleen McInerney. 2008. Recorded Books. ISBN: 9781436107242. 12 hrs. ♈

In 1911, a white family in Pluto, North Dakota, was murdered, and three innocent Indians from the nearby Ojibwe reservation were hung for the crime. Decades later, as the town is dying, their stories are still told by descendants in this now culturally blended town; and each retelling resonates and adds to the layers of their tangled history. James and McInerney capture the lyrical, cadenced language; the vibrant images; and the complex characters as the book explores themes of guilt and redemption with intelligence and even humor.

Literary Fiction; Family Saga; Multicultural Fiction.

▶ Lahiri, Jhumpa

The Namesake. Read by Sarita Choudhury. 2003. Books on Tape. ISBN: 0736695300. 10 hrs. ⓎⒶ ☙

This first novel explores the story of a name and a culture. Gogol Ganguli hopes to escape his Bengali heritage and live an American life. However, in

Lahiri's graceful, detail-rich, and evocative tale, one's identity extends beyond a name. Choudhury's reading is so comfortable and confiding that listeners are quickly drawn into the characters and their stories. She fluidly bridges the divide between worlds—between parents and children as well as between cultures—and unfamiliar phrases and customs begin to feel familiar, as do the characters and their stories.

Literary Fiction; Family Saga; Multicultural Fiction.

Morrison, Toni

Beloved. Read by Toni Morrison. 2006. Books on Tape. ISBN: 9781415935354. 12 hrs. ♛ Y A ⍉

Sometimes the author's reading of her own work transforms our experience and understanding of the novel. That happens with this mesmerizing reading by Nobel Prize–winner Morrison. Not a professional reader, she doesn't provide precise and dramatic inflections. Instead she imbues each image and phrase with her own understanding of this story of how a woman manages to live with a tragic secret from her past. Details of slavery and escape, of the Civil War and beyond, and of our country's long history of racial discrimination fill this narrative that combines a ghost story and a murder in a lyrically written, very personal tragedy.

Literary Fiction; Classic; Multicultural Fiction.

Nguyen, Bich Minh

Short Girls. Read by Alice H. Kennedy. 2009. Brilliance Audio. ISBN: 9781423391036. 8.5 hrs.

This delightful, perceptive look at assimilation issues and the immigrant experience is expressed through the candid voices of estranged Vietnamese-American sisters in Michigan. Although one is a lawyer and the other has been less motivated professionally, both face surprisingly similar issues—and being short is at the heart of them all. Kennedy's softly accented and low-key delivery allows the underlying humor to shine through, as she portrays the young women and their father, a fearless inventor who has finally claimed citizenship. An engaging and upbeat exploration of universal family issues.

Literary Fiction; Family Saga.

On the Front: Action-Packed War Stories

Tales of battles and courageous derring-do find a wide audience, including fans of adventure and historical fiction as well as good storytelling. But stories of war are often about more than just battles. While the audio versions of these tales lack the pictures and maps that accompany some of the book versions, they make up for it in the intensity of the narration.

Bruchac, Joseph
Code Talker. Read by Derrick Henry. 2006. Recorded Books. ISBN: 9781428165717. 6 hrs. Ⓨ Ⓐ

Telling the story behind how he received his war medal to his grandchildren, code talker Ned Begay relates the story of his World War II military service in this engaging and inspirational account. Narrator Henry's facility with the Navajo language and the cadence of the speech enhances this intimate, first-person novel. We listeners are held entranced by the Native American storyteller and his tales of growing up at a white-run school, required to forget his native language, and then required by the U.S. military to remember and use it in the Pacific theater. Details of Native American life in the early 20th century and the horrors of war fill this thoughtful narrative, a book for all ages.

Historical Fiction; Military Fiction; Coming-of-Age; Family Listening; Multicultural Fiction.

▶ **Cornwell, Bernard**
Agincourt. Read by Charles Keating. 2009. Books on Tape. ISBN: 9781415962640. 16 hrs. ♛

Keating's compelling narration places readers firmly on the muddy, bloody fields of France in this moving account of the famous battle in which the archers won the day for the outnumbered English. Appropriately, the chronicle's brooding hero is an archer, haunted by his conscience and the voice of St. Crispinian. In the novel and the historical note at the end, Cornwell and Keating take listeners to 1415 France and the military campaign that changed warfare forever. A dark, gritty tone emphasizes the antiwar message and adds depth to the character and his story.

Historical Fiction; Adventure; Military Fiction.

Heller, Joseph
Catch-22. Read by Jay O. Sanders. 2008. Recorded Books. ISBN: 9781436121613. 20 hrs.

Heller's contemporary classic war (or perhaps antiwar) novel may be as familiar as the catchword title, but Sanders makes the most of the marvelous, hilarious language and dialog in this smashing recording. Captain Yossarian and his comrades, based on an island near Italy, play out and attempt to escape their war responsibilities in these frighteningly believable escapades. Sanders sets up the humor in the story by skillfully capturing the cadence of the speech of men and officers. Although it has always been a good read, the dialog is so much more believable, or perhaps unbelievable, when heard. This is a book worth reading again—or listening to in this fine recording.

Literary Fiction; War Stories; Classic.

Pressfield, Steven
Gates of Fire. Read by George Guidall. 1998. Recorded Books. ISBN: 9781428153141. 18 hrs.

This intimate, first-person account of the Battle of Thermopylae tells of the 300 Spartans and a few hundred allies who held off Xerxes' thousands of warriors for days, long enough to force the king to have second thoughts about his plan of conquest. Xeones, a Spartan survivor of that momentous battle, is brought before the king and asked for his story. What he tells is more than an account of a battle, it's the tale of a young man without a city who finds a place among these fierce soldiers. He tells Xerxes of the culture that created such men, warriors who fought not for themselves but for their comrades and their city. And while they all perished there at the Hot Gates, they stopped Xerxes and his push to conquer the world. A victory in the end. Seasoned narrator George Guidall's dark baritone enhances the elegiac, bittersweet, and emotionally charged tone. He captures the cadence of the words and the epic feel of the story—as if it were written to be read aloud. A powerful, inspirational tale, well read.

Historical Fiction; Adventure; Military Fiction.

Shaara, Jeff

The Steel Wave. **Second World War Series.** Read by Paul Michael. 2008. Books on Tape. ISBN: 9781415948163. 21 hrs. 🏆 🐛

Reader Michael disappears into the characters in this detail-rich tale of preparations for D-day, and his skill with accents allows the myriad characters to speak for themselves, whether with German, English, French, or American accents. His tone underlines the drama of the event as well as the endless preparations that were made, and even though we know the outcome, we wait breathlessly as we hear about the factors that endanger the plan: from weather delays to Rommel's unexpected absence when he could have made a difference. Characters star in this deadly drama, from the generals to the enlisted men, and each personality stands out. One needn't be a fan of war stories to be absolutely riveted by this compelling account.

Historical Fiction; Adventure; Military Fiction.

Willocks, Tim

The Religion. **Tannhauser Trilogy.** Read by Simon Vance. 2006. Audio Renaissance. ISBN: 9781427201003. 25 hrs. 🏆

Vance takes readers on a day-by-day account of the Siege of Malta in 1565 in this first of the Tannhauser Trilogy. Hero Mattias Tannhauser, sword for hire, is enlisted by a French countess to find and retrieve her son, who has become involved in the epic siege. Violence, both on the battlefield and in torture chambers, dominates this cinematic tale, and it is contrasted with a stylized, formal language that reflects the speech of the times. Voicing dozens of characters, all with distinctive accents, Vance makes us intimate with the large cast and participants in the battles as well as the daily lives of everyday people under siege.

Historical Fiction; Adventure; Military Fiction.

Those Left Behind: On the Home Front

Not all wartime action takes place on the battlefield. Those left behind must supply the fighters and carry on, often in straitened circumstances. While these stories from the home front in World War II may lack the frontline horror and tragedy of war, they reveal other hardships and dangers.

Berg, Elizabeth
Dream When You're Feeling Blue. Read by Elizabeth Berg. 2007. Books on Tape. ISBN: 9781415938577. 10 hrs. ☜

In this engaging tale set in Chicago during the 1940s, Berg provides myriad details of the home front: rationing, letter writing to soldiers abroad, and the change in the work force as women take over jobs and professions formerly held by men. Berg's soft voice reflects the nostalgic tone of the novel, a comfortable tale of another time, but she also realistically voices the characters of the women who rose out of these times, independent women not content with a future filled only with family responsibilities. A gentle tale of a tumultuous time and its aftermath.

Women's Fiction; Coming-of-Age; Historical Fiction; War Stories.

Blake, Sarah
The Postmistress. Read by Orlagh Cassidy. 2010. Blackstone Audio. ISBN: 9781441725714. 11 hrs. ☜

Blake's intimate glimpse of life in 1940 intertwines the stories of three women, one in London during the Blitz and two on Cape Cod as the United States stands poised to enter the war. Postmaster (as she insists is her proper title) Iris James and the doctor's young bride Emma Fitch are captivated by American reporter Frankie Bard's astonishing radio broadcasts from London and Europe. On Cape Cod, where they live, concerned residents watch for German submarines and argue about the necessity of fighting as life goes on. Cassidy's compelling reading suits this emotionally charged, bittersweet story perfectly, underlining both the action and the growing sense of foreboding. She carefully characterizes the main and secondary characters and makes their crises both personal and universal. Her lyrical soprano evokes the poignancy of that final year before America entered the war.

Historical Fiction; Women's Fiction; War Stories.

▶ **Dallas, Sandra**
Tallgrass. Read by Lorelei King. 2007. Sound Library/BBC Audiobooks America. ISBN: 9780792746874. 8.5 hrs. ♟ ♛ Ⓨ Ⓐ ☜

When a Japanese internment camp is established in her farm community in eastern Colorado, teenager Rennie Stroud is caught up in the controversy. Feelings run high. Many townspeople are upset, and violence ensues with tragic results. Guided by her father's solid moral core, Rennie observes the conflicts with clear-eyed reason and counters the prejudice, as she comes to terms with equally pressing issues in her own family. King's heartfelt reading captures the cadence and essence of this engaging protagonist, as well as that of the generations of characters who swirl around her from townspeople and farmers to the

displaced Japanese. This ultimately hopeful, homespun tale explores the ways a distant war infiltrates family life back home. Thoughtful and heartwarming.
Historical Fiction; Coming-of-Age; Women's Fiction; War Stories.

Griner, Paul

The German Woman. Read by Anne Flosnik and Michael Page. 2009. Brilliance Audio. ISBN: 9781423392002. 12 hrs.

Griner's compelling tale of Kate Zweig and Claus Murphy presents a haunting picture of war-time life, primarily in London during World War II. Both characters have endured disturbing pasts. An Englishwoman and the widow of a German doctor, Kate served in Germany in World War I and suffered the ravages of postwar Germany. Claus is an American filmmaker, jailed for treason for making a film that threatened U.S./U.K. relations. Now he makes films in London and serves as an air warden during the nighttime raids. He's also a double agent who sends false information about D-day to the Germans. Or is he? Flosnik and Page accurately evoke the complexity of the characters and the lyrical prose. They excel at projecting the gritty, unsentimental tone of this evocative and moody novel that raises questions of loyalty and morality but provides no easy answers.
Historical Fiction; Political Thriller; War Stories.

Otsuka, Julie

When the Emperor Was Divine. Read by Elaina Erika Davis. 2003. Random House Audio. ISBN: 0739307916. 3.5 hrs. ⓨⒶ 🕮

For some Americans, the home front was as dangerous as the war zone. Otsuka's minimalist prose and unsentimental account portray a Japanese-American family from California, uprooted when the father is arrested and the mother, daughter, and son are sent to an internment camp in Utah. The contrast between what the family left behind—and ultimately lost—and the way they were then forced to live will take the listener's breath away. Davis relates the story from the perspective of each unnamed family member and reads the haunting, elegant prose in a perfectly matter-of-fact voice, which intensifies the sense of outrage and injustice. As provocative as it is evocative, this performance stuns with its simplicity.
Historical Fiction; Coming-of-Age; War Stories.

Adventure with a Purpose: The Quest

Quests have always been a popular motif, and contemporary adventure stories following the pattern of Dan Brown's blockbuster novel *The Da Vinci Code* and fantasies like J.R.R. Tolkien's *The Lord of the Rings* have kept interest high. Some quests are serious, others involve treasure, and all are stories of adventure and derring-do, well told.

Benioff, David
City of Thieves. Read by Ron Perlman. 2008. Blackstone Audiobooks. ISBN: 9781433247491. 8.5 hrs. ♆ Y A ☙

Sometimes the only way to save one's life involves a quest for something that seems insignificant. Perlman leads listeners through the deserted streets of 1941 St. Petersburg, where young Lev Benioff is arrested for looting and thrown in the most notorious of jails where he awaits his execution. Here he meets the flamboyant Kolya, a deserter and ladies' man, a bigger-than-life mentor who secures their release and their mission: to find a dozen eggs for a wedding cake for an important colonel's daughter. Under siege for weeks, St. Petersburg now likely holds no eggs, so they're off to the countryside to discover their prize. Along the way, Lev realizes, among other things, that family is where you make it in this inspirational, humorous, yet poignant coming-of-age tale. Perlman's reading showcases Kolya's bigger-than-life personality and traces Lev's education on this journey of discovery amidst a slew of eccentric characters.

Adventure; Historical Fiction; Coming-of-Age; War Stories.

Chabon, Michael
Gentlemen of the Road: A Tale of Adventure. Read by Andre Braugher. 2007. Books on Tape. ISBN: 9781415944585. 6.25 hrs.

Even Pulitzer Prize–winning authors can have fun, and Chabon does just that with this delightful adventure, originally published as a story titled "Jews with Swords." A Frankish Jew and a large African, 10th-century confidence tricksters and swords for hire, attempt to return a kidnapped prince, who turns out to be a princess, to the shores of the Caspian Sea. Braugher's exuberant reading captures every playful nuance and adds to the pure entertainment value of this swashbuckling tale.

Adventure; Historical Fiction; Humor.

Foer, Jonathan Safran
Extremely Loud and Incredibly Close. Read by Jeff Woodman, Richard Ferrone, and Barbara Caruso. 2005. Recorded Books. ISBN: 1419338919. 11 hrs. ♆ Y A ☙

Nine-year-old Oskar Schell lost his father on September 11, and now he is looking for what his father might have left him. Woodman's narration dominates this character-centered tale of long, intertwined stories of people's lives, with Ferrone and Caruso portraying Oskar's grandparents. By highlighting humor and pathos, as well as richly dramatic characters and their stories, Woodman, Ferrone, and Caruso create a magical performance. Yet it is more than just another 9/11 book. It also explores the relationship of fathers and sons, the nature of quests and what one discovers, the impact of disasters, and the importance of memories. Complex, layered, and provocative, this elegantly written story is enormously effective on audio.

Literary Fiction; Coming-of-Age; Disaster.

▶ **Lackey, Mercedes, and James Mallory**
The Phoenix Unchained. **Enduring Flame Series.** Read by William Dufris. 2007. Tantor Media. ISBN: 9781400105748. 13.5 hrs. Y A

Tiercel and Harrier live in a world where magic has all but disappeared, but when the two discover they possess strong magical powers, they must seek out those who can teach them how to harness these strengths. At the same time, the world is threatened by the Dark, as a charismatic leader preaches that Light is evil. It's hard to imagine a better reader for this entertaining coming-of-age quest than Dufris. His voice resonates with passion, enthusiasm, horror, and humor—whatever mood besets this pair on their adventures. Witty dialog, engaging characters, arduous tasks, and a relentless pace set up this series in a fascinating world where humans, elves, dragons, unicorns, and more co-exist.

Adventure; Fantasy.

Mosse, Kate
Labyrinth. Read by Donada Peters. 2006. Books on Tape. ISBN: 1415927944. 19.5 hrs. ♔

This complex adventure tale offers story lines in the present and in 13th-century France, as two women—Alice in the present and Alais in the past—become entangled in dangerous intrigues to protect the Grail. Alice Tanner, a volunteer on a dig, discovers two skeletons and a ring carved with an elaborate labyrinth, and her life is suddenly endangered by sinister characters, while the historical Alais and her crusader father struggle to safeguard the Grail. Peters provides a strong sense of foreboding and menace in both time periods and keeps listeners anxiously awaiting every plot twist. Her graceful narration integrates the profuse and authentic historical details with the fascinating tidbits of the Grail legend, as she deftly portrays characters' thoughts and emotions.

Adventure; Historical Fiction.

Reading the Bones: Forensic Evidence

When Patricia Cornwell published her first mystery filled with forensic details, none of us imagined it would become such a hot topic—in books, television, and film. Forensic evidence now plays a major role in much fiction and nonfiction, and these titles focus on the intricate details of forensic science.

Bass, William M., and Jon Jefferson
Death's Acre: Inside the Legendary Forensic Lab, the Body Farm, Where the Dead Do Tell Tales. Read by George Grizzard and Bill Bass. 2003. Simon & Schuster Audio. ISBN: 0743534026. 6 hrs. Nonfiction. ☕

Although abridged, this recording highlights Bass's greatest career accomplishment—the Body Farm, the lab that has provided the scientific information fueling our knowledge of forensics. Bass, a natural storyteller, relates the true history of the Body Farm, as well as his own adventures as an anthropologist often employed by law enforcement to decipher bones and bodies. Grizzard clearly relishes the material and makes an affable guide through the sometimes grisly subject.

Popular Science.

Cornwell, Patricia Daniels

Postmortem. **Kay Scarpetta Series**. Read by C. J. Critt. 1993. Recorded Books. ISBN: 0788744631. 11.5 hrs. ♈

The enormous popularity of Cornwell's medical examiner Kay Scarpetta changed the mystery and thriller genres. In this first volume in the long-running series, Scarpetta's forensic investigation brings her to the attention of a serial murderer and puts her in grave danger. Several different narrators have read titles in this series, but here Texan Critt's light tones create a credible heroine, and she excels in setting the mood of danger and menace.

Mystery; Suspense; Thriller.

Franklin, Ariana

Mistress of the Art of Death. **Adelia Aguilar Series.** Read by Rosalyn Landor. 2007. Books on Tape. ISBN: 9781415936986. 13.25 hrs. ♈

When the Jews of 12th-century Cambridge are blamed for the deaths of four Catholic children, King Henry II imports a forensic expert from Sicily to discover the cause of death and protect the Jews, the group most amenable to loaning him funds to keep the country afloat. Enter Dr. Adelia Aguilar, the mistress of the title, who lets the dead speak but who must pretend to be the assistant of her manservant, since a woman physician would never be accepted or believed. Landor voices a diverse cast of characters—Adelia and her group, crusaders back from the wars, locals from the fens—from a wide range of regions and social classes. She depicts a believable, introspective heroine who faces the challenges of culture, gender, and murder investigation with aplomb. Landor is wonderfully effective in conveying the mood, which often reflects the dark and edgy nature of the violent times, and she also presents an accurately detailed picture of medieval life in Cambridge, where issues of race, class, gender, and religion created drama in everyday events. This is the first in the series, although later titles have different narrators.

Mystery; Historical Fiction.

▶ Johansen, Iris

The Face of Deception. **Eve Duncan Novels**. Read by Laurel Lefkow. 2002. BBC Audiobooks America. ISBN: 9780792727521. 11 hrs. [Y][A]

In this first in a long-running series, forensic sculptor Eve Duncan is asked by a computer mogul to reconstruct a murder victim's skull. What seems a simple job turns out to be fraught with danger. Lefkow conveys both the heart-pounding suspense and the heartrending details of Eve's past: her only daughter Bonnie was murdered by a serial killer. Subsequently, Eve has devoted her career to reconstructing the skulls of murdered children, a pursuit later installments reveal can be equally dangerous. A touch of the paranormal (Bonnie's ghost appears to comfort and assist), adrenaline-spiked pacing, and sympathetic characters add to these suspenseful tales, rich in forensic details.

Suspense; Mystery.

Reichs, Kathy

Bones to Ashes. **Temperance Brennan Mysteries.** Read by Barbara Rosenblat. 2007. Recorded Books. ISBN: 9781428153578. 10.5 hrs.

Forensic anthropologist Temperance (Tempe) Brennan divides her life and work between Montreal, Quebec, in the equivalent of a coroner's office, and North Carolina, where she is an anthropology professor and consults for the medical examiner's office. In this, the 10th in the series, she confronts bones of a child found in New Brunswick. Could they belong to her long-ago best friend who disappeared when Tempe was a child? More bones of adolescents lead to unsettling possibilities. The mix of cultures (French Canadian and U.S.), sometimes gruesome forensic details, complex investigations, building suspense, and intriguing characters make this a not-to-be missed series that provides an excellent stage for the talents of reader Rosenblat. Her flawless accents and expressive reading enhance these compelling mysteries, filled with humor and heart.

Mystery; Suspense.

Roach, Mary

Stiff: The Curious Life of Human Cadavers. Read by Shelly Frasier. 2003. Tantor Media. ISBN: 1400100976. 7 hrs. Nonfiction. [Y][A]

Fans of forensic details may also appreciate this quirky nonfiction exploration of the uses of cadavers. Mixing humor with respect, this unexpectedly informative and well-researched title amuses and enlightens. Frasier's narration captures Roach's sophisticated and often irreverent style, and despite the seriousness of some of the chapters and material, it's impossible occasionally not to laugh out loud. The book is full of fascinating facts about the history of cadavers, as well as the way they are used now to help the living. If the fictional accounts of forensics freak you out, try this as an antidote.

Humor; Popular Science.

Of Mythic Proportions: Retelling Classic Tales

Tales from childhood sometimes find new life when reimagined and retold. Familiar stories and characters set in other times and places often resonate with readers because these tales invoke the old and known with the added piquancy of the new and unusual.

▶ **Connolly, John**
The Book of Lost Things. Read by Stephen Crossley. 2006. Recorded Books. ISBN: 9781428120471. 11 hrs. Y A

When his mother dies, young David takes refuge in the books she left him. Then the books begin to speak and lure him into another world where fairy tales have come to life, but those watered-down characters from childhood tales now loom large and malevolent. Like Dorothy in *The Wonderful Wizard of Oz*, he goes in search of a king who owns the eponymous book that will help him find his way home. His quest is fraught with dangers and terror at every turn, but David is helped by new friends when he least expects it. Crossley makes this fantastic world and its denizens real. His voice conveys both the menacing tone and the true character of the players, as well as their words. An enchanting coming-of-age tale set in a magical nightmare world.

Fantasy; Coming-of-Age; Humor; Quest; Family Listening.

Fforde, Jasper
The Big Over Easy: A Nursery Crime. **Nursery Crime Series.** Read by Simon Prebble. 2005. BBC Audiobooks America. ISBN: 0792737016. 12 hrs.

It's Easter time in Reading, England, but another Reading, ingeniously transformed, where Inspector Jack Spratt and his able assistant Mary Mary are called in to investigate the death of Humpty Stuyvesant Van Dumpty III, minor Baronet, ex-con, and former philanthropist. Was this an accident or murder? Spratt must solve the case to save the department and his job, so he's off on an investigation that involves a host of nursery rhyme characters, all newly imagined and not quite so benign as we remember. Prebble proves the perfect companion for this leisurely investigative stroll among the nursery crimes and criminals. His debonair delivery and nuanced tone underline the deadpan humor and literate whimsy in Fforde's lampooning of mystery and fantasy genres alike. A treat for the ears.

Fantasy; Mystery; Humor.

Gardner, John
Grendel. Read by George Guidall. 1997. Recorded Books. ISBN: 9781402551109. 5.5 hrs. Y A

Gardner reimagines *Beowulf* from the monster's point of view in this engaging retelling that adopts the high language of epic poetry but adds a large dose of wit. In a gruff and grumbling voice, Guidall navigates the dense prose with ease and allows the underlying humor to emerge, as he relates the tale of a momma's boy who ravages the land but also has a brain and a heart. No longer the mindless evil of the epic, this legendary monster turns out to be an unexpectedly introspective antihero with a philosophical bent. An interesting take on a classic heroic tale. Guidall also narrated Heaney's translation of *Beowulf*, annotated under the "Lasting Pleasures: Classics Come Alive" heading in this chapter.

Fantasy; Literary Fiction.

Maguire, Gregory

Mirror, Mirror. Read by John McDonough, Kate Forbes, Barbara Rosenblat, and Richard Ferrone. 2003. Recorded Books. ISBN: 9781402567865. 9 hrs. ☙

What if Snow White's story were set against the backdrop of political intrigues in 16th-century Italy? Maguire adopts just that scenario in this marvelous multicast recording that places young Bianca in the hands of Lucrezia Borgia. McDonough carries the narration in his rich, slightly gruff voice, with the others performing first-person sections from various characters' points of view. All combine to create an intriguing revisionist fairy tale, as real politics and personalities blend seamlessly with the imaginary in ways that make both more believable.

Fantasy; Historical Fiction.

McKinley, Robin

Sunshine. Read by Laural Merlington. 2008. Tantor Media. ISBN: 9781400110087. 15.5 hrs. ♛ Y A

McKinley recasts the classic tale of Beauty and the Beast in an urban fantasy setting after the Voodoo Wars when most cities were destroyed. Rae Seddon, known as Sunshine, tells her own story of her encounter with dark forces that led to the discovery of her magical powers as the daughter of a legendary sorcerer. But it is a despised vampire who helps her understand her magical legacy. Merlington uses her expressive voice to enrich and inhabit characters and story. Despite the sinister atmosphere, this is a warm and fuzzy urban fantasy, with lyrical prose and a charming narrator.

Fantasy; Coming-of-Age.

The Real Story: Exceptional Nonfiction Recordings

Early recordings of nonfiction audiobooks were often less than stellar. Flat narration of facts did not generate many fans. More recently, skilled narrators and fascinating stories combine to make exceptional listening experiences.

Ambrose, Stephen E.

Band of Brothers: E Company, 506th Regiment, 101st Airborne from Normandy to Hitler's Eagle's Nest. Read by Tim Jerome. 2003. BBC Audiobooks America. ISBN: 0792799321. 13 hrs. Nonfiction.

Ambrose interweaves authentic details of battles, character studies based on interviews and documents, and action scenes in this character-centered nonfiction account of a World War II Parachute Infantry Regiment from their training camp in 1944 through Normandy and beyond. What the audio version lacks in visuals—maps and photographs—it makes up for with the you-are-there sense of immediacy. Jerome's matter-of-fact narration underlines the immensity of the odds the soldiers faced and the straightforward getting on with the task that characterized these men. This inspirational story, rich in historical details but told through the lives of the soldiers, offers insights specifically into the lives of World War II soldiers but also into the life of any wartime soldier.

History; Adventure; Military History.

Capote, Truman
In Cold Blood. Read by Scott Brick. 2006. Books on Tape. ISBN: 1415930929. 14.5 hrs. Nonfiction. ♛ Y A ☙

This classic "nonfiction novel" presents a 1959 crime—the killing of the Clutter family in western Kansas—and the subsequent search for the killers and their trial. Capote combines reporting with dramatic character portraits, and Brick performs this blend seamlessly, letting the power of the story shine. Colorful, dramatic, and compelling, this gripping true tale still chills in both the telling of the crime and the examination of the murderers. Brick displays the passions and motivations of the characters on both sides of the law, and he instills the book, originally published in 1965, with new life.

True Crime.

Grisham, John
The Innocent Man: Murder and Justice in a Small Town. Read by Craig Wasson. 2006. Books on Tape. ISBN: 9781415933077. 12.5 hrs. Nonfiction.

Better known for his fictional legal thrillers, Grisham tackles a true miscarriage of justice here. Wasson narrates this nonfiction account, filled with newspaper and court reports, in a straightforward fashion, documenting how poor legal representation and inadequate police work drove an innocent man to insanity. Details of the families, the crime, and the long legal wrangles make for a compelling story—but unlike Grisham's fiction, it is not one in which the author can make things right.

True Crime.

▶ Kurson, Robert
Shadow Divers: The True Adventure of Two Americans Who Risked Everything to Solve One of the Last Mysteries of World War II. Read by Michael Prichard. 2004. Books on Tape. ISBN: 1415902836. 16.5 hrs. Nonfiction. ♛ Y A ☙

Intrigue, mystery, and danger fill this compelling nonfiction tale of the discovery of a previously unidentified German submarine off the coast of New Jersey. Prichard navigates the rich detail—of deep diving, of submarine life, of military history—and embodies a range of fascinating characters, as he recounts the adventures of the divers as well as of the German sailors and their families.

His mesmerizing reading of this riveting action-packed tale creates an edge-of-the chair listening experience. Many a driveway moment.

Adventure; History.

Philbrick, Nathaniel

In the Heart of the Sea: The Tragedy of the Whaleship Essex. Read by Scott Brick. 2000. Books on Tape. ISBN: 0736659722. 10.5 hrs. Nonfiction. ♈ Y A

Relying on actual documents, especially survivor accounts, Philbrick offers the nonfiction tale of the disastrous sinking of a 240-ton whaler by a sperm whale, the event that became the basis for Herman Melville's classic novel, *Moby Dick*. Brick voices this absorbing account with just the right measure of foreboding (the men sense the impending disaster and listeners know what lies ahead) and calm, objective recounting of gutwrenching detail. Characters take top billing, and Brick's reading brings them to the fore, while filling in tales of derring-do, cannibalism, and rescue. Philbrick offers intriguing details of the whaling industry and Nantucket's commercial, social, and religious character, which Brick handles well. But Brick also recognizes the value of a good tale of adventure and survival, and he makes the most of this thrilling story.

History; Adventure.

Timely Tales: Fiction Ripped from the Headlines

It's one thing to read the newspapers, it's quite another to be taken inside these stories through the art of audiobooks. These titles tackle topics we read about every day, but hearing about them makes them very real and personal—and all the more possible and terrifying.

Baldacci, David

The Camel Club. **Camel Club Series.** Read by Jonathan Davis. 2005. Books on Tape. ISBN: 1415925186. 16 hrs.

Conspiracy within the government and without, terrorists threatening, the fate of the United States at stake—what's not to like in this first of Baldacci's series of alienated misfits, living off the grid, but having vast resources (intellectual, computer, and even monetary) to draw on in their fight to save the world. Narrator Davis inhabits this quirky cast of characters, good guys we care about and bad guys we love to hate. He leads listeners through this complex, often-violent, and thoughtful thriller, with plots twists and action in every chapter as well as a probing consideration of the troubling issues. Satisfyingly claustrophobic.

Thriller.

Box, C.J.
Below Zero. **Joe Pickett Series.** Read by David Chandler. 2009. Recorded Books. ISBN: 9781440755064. 10.5 hrs.

A new kind of eco-terrorist, determined to punish those whose carbon footprints loom too large (the title refers to an ecologist's ideal of living with a "below zero" carbon footprint, or in other words, living in a way that actually makes a positive impact on the environment), invades Wyoming game warden Joe Pickett's territory and brings mayhem and death—along with the possibility that his adopted daughter, long thought dead, is really alive. The environmental message drives the plot, but Chandler's performance underlines the darkly unsettling mood and the growing suspense. He makes the politics of green personal and very dangerous, but he never neglects the series characters and especially the introspective hero's ruminations, actions, and fears. An interesting counterpoint of the universal and the personal, set against a beautifully evoked Western landscape.

Mystery; Suspense; Western.

Coben, Harlan
Hold Tight. Read by Scott Brick. 2008. Brilliance. ISBN: 9781423327493. 12 hrs.

Coben writes the kind of book Brick was born to narrate with edge-of-the-seat suspense, tension building to nightmare proportions, and characters we care about. These novels deal with the everyday and ordinary, which makes them all the more frightening. Here he adds provocative issues directly from the nightly news—computer spyware used by both bad guys and parents, privacy issues, parental responsibility, and children placed in jeopardy. Multiple storylines require Brick to flip back and forth, building tension and terror. He ramps up the relentless pacing and unflagging sense of unease, and his impassioned reading makes the dangers seem all too close to home.

Suspense.

▶ **Deaver, Jeffery**
The Broken Window. **Lincoln Rhyme Series.** Read by George Guidall. 2008. Recorded Books. ISBN: 9781436118576. 14 hrs.

Yikes! If you've got any fears about identity theft, you might want to pass on this eighth installment in Deaver's popular Lincoln Rhyme series. Guidall's voice is perfect, both as the familiar series characters and as the sinister, creepy murderer who manipulates data base information to implicate innocent people. Guidall provides the step-by-step scoop on the data mining and framing, all the while establishing the dramatic and claustrophobic tone. If even Rhyme and his crew can be hit, is anyone safe?

Suspense; Thriller; Mystery.

Smith, Martin Cruz
Wolves Eat Dogs. **Arkady Renko Series.** Read by Henry Strozier. 2005. Recorded Books. ISBN: 1419315781. 12 hrs.

In the aftermath of the Chernobyl nuclear disaster and in a Russia ruled by new faces and new problems, Moscow policeman Arkady Renko is called in to investigate a suicide that leads him to the deadly Zone of Exclusion, the area of radiation surrounding Chernobyl. Strozier's edgy, gravelly voice embodies aging Renko's persona, cynical and yet always curious, introspective and empathetic, a man who has struggled with the old Russia and now the new. Strozier guides listeners through this complex, layered plot, projecting the evocative and foreboding tone, the rich characterizations, and the elegant language.

Mystery; Thriller.

Updike, John
Terrorist. Read by Christopher Lane. 2006. Brilliance Audio. ISBN: 9781423318637. 10 hrs. Y A ☙

Lane accurately captures both characters and tone in this edgy and provocative examination of a disillusioned 18-year-old, half-Irish and half-Egyptian high school student who has been offered the opportunity to perform a terrorist act. Updike's stylish prose lends itself perfectly to audio in its unhurried yet compelling detail, as he probes the psychological motivations of his protagonist. Lane's portrayal keeps us at arm's length, allowing listeners to observe the intriguing characters as they play out their lives in Updike's 21st-century America, a country forever changed by the events on September 11, 2001.

Literary Fiction; Thriller.

Under Occupation: War Stories

The dangers of war don't exist solely on the front. People under occupation by an enemy force continue to face dangers every day. How they cope and the qualities that are revealed make some of the best stories, fiction and nonfiction.

Ackerman, Diane
The Zookeeper's Wife: A War Story. Read by Suzanne Toren. 2007. BBC Audiobooks America. ISBN: 9780792750185. 11 hrs. Nonfiction. ♆ ☙

When the Warsaw Zoo was occupied by the Nazis and the best animals were shipped to German zoos, Jan and Antonina Zabinski husbanded supplies and resources to keep the remaining animals alive—and then, in a move of fearless bravery, they turned the zoo into a hotbed of insurgency and a storage depot for weapons and refugees. This is a story of personalities, and through Toren's skilled vocalizations, an astounding range of people and animals live in our imaginations. Toren's dramatic reading captures the inspirational as well as the comic elements in this lyrical, life-affirming true story of selfless courage and ingenuity in the face of the horrors of war.

War Stories.

Gies, Miep

Anne Frank Remembered: The Story of the Woman Who Helped to Hide the Frank Family. Read by Barbara Rosenblat. 2009. Oasis. ISBN: 9781598595239. 9 hrs. Nonfiction.

Gies's memoir adds another layer to the tragic story of Anne Frank and her family with this gripping account of those who sheltered the family for 25 months, hidden within a secret annex. This memoir provides fascinating details about Gies, Otto Frank's secretary, and her husband, as well as the Frank family and the events that led to their capture. Rosenblat embraces the Dutch cadences and accent in this marvelous chronicle of courage in wartime. Each character comes vibrantly to life in her skilled performance, and the stark realities of occupied Amsterdam as well as the emotional intensity of the true story make this a memorable book and performance.

Memoir; War Stories.

Némirovsky, Irène

Suite Française. Read by Daniel Oreskes and Barbara Rosenblat. 2006. HighBridge Audio. ISBN: 1598870203. 13.25 hrs.

In these riveting first two stories of a planned quintet covering the German occupation of France from 1940, Némirovsky, who was killed at Auschwitz in 1942, brings an authentic sense of immediacy to her semiautobiographical tales of Parisians escaping Paris as the Wehrmacht approaches. Oreskes reads the first story, "Storm in June," in a lovely baritone that hooks and holds listeners as he recounts the stories of Parisians of all classes in flight. Rosenblat's understated performance of "Dolce" offers additional character studies of French and Germans alike, making their way together in the interlude before the Germans invaded Russia. The close proximity of French and Germans after the battles leads to a new sense of community; collaboration with the enemy becomes natural and thus much more insidious. Elegantly written, polished prose lends itself to a poignant and haunting audio performance, enriched by black humor and irony.

Literary Fiction; War Stories.

Russell, Mary Doria

A Thread of Grace. Read by Cassandra Campbell. 2005. Books on Tape. ISBN: 1415916470. 20 hrs.

In 1943 many Jews sought sanctuary in northwest Italy, and thousands were saved by Italians, despite Germany's best efforts to destroy them. Russell relates this little-known piece of history through the eyes of a large cast of engaging characters—Jews and Catholics, peasants and nobility, resistance fighters and refugees. Faced with a vast cast and multiple European accents, Campbell offers an expressive reading that reveals the hearts of the characters, good and bad, and places listeners in the midst of history in this heartwarming saga. A riveting performance of this story of violence, danger, and tragedy.

Historical Fiction; Literary Fiction; War Stories.

▶ **Simon, Scott**
Pretty Birds. Read by Christina Moore. 2005. Recorded Books. ISBN: 9781419340604. 14 hrs. Ⓨ Ⓐ

When the home front becomes the war front, life changes on many levels. A teenage girl, a high school basketball star in Sarajevo, becomes a sniper in the ongoing war between Muslims and Christians. As in America's Civil War, friend becomes foe, neighbors struggle against each other, and religious politics drive the action. Moore's haunting reading grabs listeners from the beginning and leaves an indelible impression on our consciousness, even years after hearing it. Not only does she inhabit the characters, her reading reflects both the political reality and the moody undertones of events. Heartfelt, gritty, and provocative. Every word rings true.

Literary Fiction; Coming-of-Age; War Stories.

Chapter Four

Characters

For many readers and listeners, characters are a book's most important aspect. Audiobooks bring a host of memorable characters to life in the imagination of listeners through the added dimension of sound—adding a real voice to our mental inventions. One of the most important aspects of an audiobook, and thus the work of narrators, is the creation of character voices, and many narrators pride themselves on their interpretative abilities as well as their skills with unique voices and accents. Narrators devise voices appropriate to gender and tone. Skilled narrators also distinguish among characters and establish them through dialects, accents, tone, and pitch. They create linguistic quirks that make characters engaging or detestable and thus enhance the listener's pleasure.

These lists introduce a quirky mix of characters—real people in fiction and nonfiction, royalty, assassins, legendary heroes and heroines, and more. All feature masterful narrators whose skill at presenting characters enlivens the stories they read.

All in the Family: Family Stories

Family stories satisfy with interesting characters and often complex relationships, because despite Tolstoy's adage that all happy families are alike, even happy families have memorable stories.

▶ **Cisneros, Sandra**
Caramelo. Read by Sandra Cisneros. 2002. BBC Audiobooks America. ISBN: 0792727355. 16 hrs. 🏆 Ⓨ Ⓐ 📚

Memorable characters, stories within stories, gorgeous prose, and lilting accents make readers feel right at home with the Reyes clan, both in Chicago and in Mexico City. Lala, the youngest daughter, directs this tale, which reveals the richness of family life—in personalities and secrets, as well as food, traditions, and family lore. Cisneros proves an excellent reader of this semiautobiographical novel, and her whimsical narration celebrates the pleasures and problems of close-knit families in the past, present, and future.

Literary Fiction; Family Saga; Multicultural Fiction.

de los Santos, Marisa

Belong to Me. Read by Julia Gibson. 2008. HarperAudio. ISBN: 9780061557637. 15.5 hrs.

When "family" expands beyond the confines of a house to include friends as well, new pressures arise in this sprawling story of intertwining lives. Cornelia and Teo move from New York to the Philadelphia suburbs, a close-knit community where they struggle to fit in and start a family. Gibson navigates domestic issues and emotions with grace, and distinguishes among the multiple points of view with pitch, cadence, and tone. Couples and friends find their loyalties stretched as they discover how life changes people and how people change with life.

Women's Fiction.

Erdrich, Louise

The Master Butchers Singing Club. Read by Louise Erdrich. 2003. BBC Audiobooks America. ISBN: 0792728637. 15.5 hrs. 📚

Erdrich narrates her own novel, an elegant family drama, told matter-of-factly and without melodrama. She tells of Fidelis Waldvogel, a German sniper who returns from the battlefields of World War I; marries his dead comrade's pregnant wife; emigrates to Argus, North Dakota; and establishes a butcher's shop and a singing club. Intertwined is the tale of Delphine Watzka, who escaped Argus and joined the circus, only to return and work for Fidelis and befriend his wife Eva. Fascinating characters, haunting images, and rich stories lend themselves to a memorable listen.

Literary Fiction; Family Saga; Historical Fiction; Multicultural Fiction.

Lipman, Elinor

The Family Man. Read by Jonathan Davis. 2009. BBC/Sound Library. ISBN: 9780792760207. 10 hrs.

Lipman's smart take on family life features gay lawyer Henry Archer who rediscovers his ex-stepdaughter Thalia and rebuilds their family in contemporary New York City. Sophisticated and heartwarming, this charming tale explores the nature of family and its sometimes unconventional makeup. Witty dialog, quirky characters, and great splashes of humor make this a pleasure for listeners. Davis excels at disappearing into the story and allowing each character to speak and to explore what makes a family.

Literary Fiction; Humor.

Quindlen, Anna
Rise and Shine. Read by Carol Monda. 2006. Recorded Books. ISBN: 1419388932.
8.75 hrs. ☃

Family issues propel Quindlen's novels, and here she offers two sisters—
Meghan, a driven television star, and Bridget, a social worker who has always
lived in Meghan's shadow. Until, that is, Meghan has an on-air meltdown and
inadvertently utters profanities into an open mike. Then it's Bridget who must
pick up the pieces, because that's what sisters do. Monda clearly differenti-
ates between the two sisters' voices and ably switches between them, perfectly
capturing the emotions—and emotional fallout—of every scene, as each sister
discovers her role and her future.

Women's Fiction; Humor.

The Good, the Bad, and the Nosey:
Amateur Sleuths

These detectives don't have licenses, but that doesn't stop them from investigating! Some are snoops, direct descendants of Agatha Christie's Miss Marple,
and others bring more traditional investigative skills. All face deadly dangers as
they are pulled into searches for the identities of murderers.

Davidson, Diane Mott
Dark Tort. **Goldy Bear Series.** Read by Barbara Rosenblat. 2006. Recorded Books.
ISBN: 1419390155. 10.5 hrs.

Crime-solving caterer Goldy Bear Schulz always seems to encounter murder in picturesque Aspen Meadow, Colorado. In this clever 13th episode, a para-
legal in the law firm where Goldy has a lucrative contract has been strangled,
and the young woman's devastated mother asks Goldy to investigate. Rosenblat
reads all the series titles with élan, personifying familiar series characters and
providing just the right edge in voicing the bad guys. Humor abounds in this
mostly cozy series, despite the sometimes violent deaths, and Goldy's recipes,
read in mouthwatering detail by Rosenblat, always steal the show. This is a
series listeners can pick up almost anywhere.

Mystery; Humor.

Francis, Dick
Under Orders. **Sid Halley Series.** Read by Martin Jarvis. 2006. Books on Tape.
ISBN: 9781415935064. 10 hrs.

Most of Francis'40-plus mysteries are stand-alone titles, and one can listen to any to get a good sense of his lively plots featuring likeable heroes and
filled with horse and racing lore. He wrote only one series, featuring jockey-
turned-detective Sid Halley, and in this fourth entry, Halley investigates three
deaths on Cheltenham Gold Cup Day. Jarvis, who has narrated many Francis

titles, conveys the essence of each character as well as the excitement of the chase and a wealth of knowledge about horse racing. Danger and violence up the stakes, and Jarvis captures it all, pulling listeners into the fray. Don't let potential listeners be put off by the horse-racing emphasis; these are all terrific mysteries, filled with splendid characters and dangerous investigations.

Mystery; Thriller.

Hart, Carolyn G.

Murder Walks the Plank: A Death on Demand Mystery. **Death on Demand Series.** Read by Kate Reading. 2004. Books on Tape. ISBN: 0736699236. 10.5 hrs.

In this 15th title in the long-running cozy series featuring Annie Darling, bookstore owner on Broward's Rock, South Carolina, Annie and husband Max embark on a mystery cruise, and while they are on the ship, one of the guests falls—or was pushed—overboard. When police call this and a subsequent suicide "accidents," Annie and her friends feel compelled to investigate. Filled with multiple references to great mystery novels (and there's even a quiz in each book), this series celebrates the genre. Series narrator Reading inhabits the characters with her wealth of diverse voices and accents, and her remarkable vocal talents allow her to capture cadences accurately and play up every bit of the humor. A delightful series that welcomes new listeners at any point.

Mystery; Humor.

Kellerman, Jonathan

Compulsion. **Alex Delaware Series.** Read by John Rubinstein. 2008. Books on Tape. ISBN: 9781415944011. 10 hrs.

Psychologist Dr. Alex Delaware once again assists LAPD Detective Milo Sturgis in solving a series of brutal murders linked by black luxury cars and expensive scarves. This 22nd case stands as a good entry point to this series characterized by the usual twisted story line, sympathetic heroes pitted against evil villains, fast-paced action, building suspense, and touches of humor. Frequent series narrator Rubinstein comfortably embodies the characters, adding a gravelly gruffness to Sturgis's voice and reflecting the cool intellectual approach favored by Delaware. He makes the most of the moody suspense, the building tension, and the witty dialog that fans love. His voice holds listeners enthralled as we wait on the edges of our chairs for the denouement.

Mystery; Suspense.

▶ Spencer-Fleming, Julia

In the Bleak Midwinter. **Reverend Clare Fergusson Series.** Read by Suzanne Toren. 2004. BBC Audiobooks America. ISBN: 0792731808. 13 hrs. ♛

Newly minted Episcopal priest Claire Fergusson, a daughter of the South, faces her first winter in Millers Kill, New York, and the arrival at her church door of a foundling during a snowstorm. Later she and police chief Russ van Alstyne discover the body of the baby's mother, and together they uncover some of the town's deadly secrets. Toren's precise and thoughtful reading reveals the complexity of the series characters and highlights the emotional underpinnings of this provocative and layered mystery, as well as the dark and uneasy tone. Toren's voice reflects Claire's slight Southern accent but also hints at the edginess her years as an Army helicopter pilot have given her. Start with this, the first book in this series, to appreciate the richly drawn characters and complex moral issues of this unusual mystery series.

Mystery.

Learning Life's Lessons:
Coming-of-Age Tales

Coming-of-age novels are popular with a wide range of listeners of all ages. The diverse group below reflects a variety of times and places but the quintessential story of learning life's lessons remains the same in all.

Doig, Ivan
The Whistling Season. Read by Jonathan Hogan. 2006. Recorded Books. ISBN: 142810111X. 12 hrs. ♈ ⓎⒶ

In this nostalgic paean to the virtues of the American West, Doig presents the Milliron family, three motherless sons raised on a ranch in the early 1900s. When their father hires a housekeeper, their lives change, especially hero Paul's as he benefits from the housekeeper's brother's unique approach to education. Forty years later Paul's memories of his one-room school education affect his decision as superintendent of public instruction in the age of Sputnik. Hogan seamlessly captures Doig's genial storytelling cadence, colorful language, evocative landscape, and haunting, elegiac tone in this heartwarming historical novel.

Coming-of-Age; Historical Fiction.

King, Stephen
Carrie. Read by Sissy Spacek. 2005. Recorded Books. ISBN: 140259383X. 7.25 hrs. ⓎⒶ

Not all coming-of-age stories leave listeners with a warm and fuzzy feeling. Some are downright terrifying! Horror giant King's first novel explores the ravages of adolescence and the power of a teenager when she comes into her own. Spacek's recent recording introduces this classic title to a new audience and reminds others of the book's power to captivate and horrify (and perhaps of Spacek's own performance in the lead role in the 1976 movie version). Her accent may be more Texas than Down East, but her powerful delivery will induce more than a few cringes and gasps.

Horror; Coming-of-Age.

Petterson, Per
Out Stealing Horses. Trans. Anne Born. Read by Richard Poe. 2008. Recorded Books. ISBN: 9781436121392. 7.25 hrs. ♈ 📚

Mourning the loss of his sister and his wife, Trond Sander moves to an isolated corner of Norway and keeps to himself—that is, until he encounters his neighbor who seems surprisingly familiar. Memories of the summer of 1948 flood back; it was a pivotal moment in his life when everything changed. Gorgeous imagery, a moody atmosphere, and haunting, spare prose fill this novel. Poe so effectively portrays both the older Sander and his boyhood self that he seems to disappear, leaving listeners spellbound by the flow of breathtaking language and story.

Literary Fiction; Coming-of-Age.

▶ **Picoult, Jodi**

My Sister's Keeper. Read by Julia Gibson, Jenny Ikeda, Barbara McCulloh, Carol Monda, Andy Paris, Richard Poe, and Tom Stechschulte. 2004. Recorded Books. ISBN: 9781402586408. 13.75 hrs. 🎧 Ⓨ Ⓐ 📖

Anna was genetically engineered to be a donor for her older sister, dying from leukemia, but at 13, she's had enough, and she seeks medical emancipation from her parents. Picoult's provocative novel was popular with general readers and especially book discussion groups before it became a major motion picture. However, this wonderfully effective reading by a full cast adds yet another layer of complexity to the story and its ramifications. Each carefully voiced role is so sympathetic that it raises even more questions about what is moral, what is ethical, and what is not. The twists in the last two discs are almost guaranteed to reduce even the hardest hearted to tears. It's unfortunate that Recorded Books did not bother to identify the roles read by each narrators.

Literary Fiction; Women's Fiction; Coming-of-Age.

Siddons, Anne Rivers

Sweetwater Creek. Read by Anna Fields. 2005. BBC Audiobooks America. ISBN: 0792737393. 11 hrs.

In this perfect confluence of reader and story, Fields presents preteen Emily Parmenter, almost forgotten after the suicide of her brother and disappearance of her mother from the family's spaniel-breeding plantation. Emily finds solace and satisfaction in training the dogs until a rebellious debutante arrives for the summer and shakes her family's world. Fields's husky alto perfectly complements the lush prose and slow pace of life in the Carolina Low Country, almost a character on its own. Each voice rings with true emotion, and Fields transports listeners to the heart of this story of a young girl's journey to self-discovery.

Women's Fiction; Coming-of-Age.

Women with Spunk: Feisty Females in Fiction

Sometimes humorous, sometimes tragic, these characters capture our imagination with their inventive strategies, expressive personalities, intelligence, and wit. Who said women are the weaker sex?

Andrews, Mary Kay
Savannah Blues. **Weezie Foley Series.** Read by Susan Ericksen. 2006. Brilliance
Audio. ISBN: 9781423323303. 13 hrs.

Undaunted by a contentious divorce, the loss of her lovely home in Savannah's historic district, and the shaky status of her antiques business, Eloise
(Weezie) Foley finds herself charged with murder when her ex-husband's girlfriend is discovered dead at an estate sale. Not only does Ericksen clearly enjoy
playing Weezie to the hilt, she also successfully gives voice to the host of eccentric friends and relatives who people this tale. Irresistible characters, over-the-top
adventures, and laugh-out-loud humor characterize this mystery and Ericksen's
winning performance.

Mystery; Women's Fiction; Humor.

Evanovich, Janet
One for the Money. **Stephanie Plum Series.** Read by C.J. Critt. 1995. Recorded
Books. ISBN: 9780788734069. 8.5 hrs. 🏆

Out of work again, Stephanie Plum turns to her cousin, a bail bondsman,
and takes a job as a bounty hunter. Hilarity ensues in this first (and all subsequent adventures) featuring our heroine and a cast of colorful characters: her
lovers (a policeman and a darkly dangerous and mysterious bounty hunter), her
sidekick Lula, and the ineffable Grandma Mazur, who never found a funeral
visitation she didn't like. Each entry in this series involves danger, adventure,
steamy romance, and madcap humor as Critt leads us through a life without a
dull moment. Judging by the humor in her voice, Critt had as much fun reading
as we do listening!

Mystery; Humor.

Fforde, Jasper
The Eyre Affair. **Thursday Next Series.** Read by Susan Duerden. 2009. Books
on Tape. ISBN: 9781415966648. 12.25 hrs. Y A

In an alternate 1985 Britain, where the Crimean War is still being fought
and books and their characters live in the everyday world, fearless Special Op-
erative Thursday Next of the Literary Detection branch fights against villains
determined to alter classic works of fiction. In this new recording, Duerden artfully captures all the characters—from the winsome Next to the evil genius and
assorted authors and quirky personalities in between—as well as the playful
sense of this madcap romp, which features endless puns, plays on words, and
literary references. Whether you read this series as fantasy, literary fiction, or
mystery, the seriously funny tone is sure to please.

Mystery; Literary Fiction; Fantasy; Humor.

Larsson, Stieg
The Girl Who Played with Fire. **Millennium Trilogy.** Read by Simon Vance. 2009.
Books on Tape. ISBN: 9781415964361. 18.5 hrs.

Vance's cool, dark British accent highlights the drama of characters and
events in this second mystery by the late Larsson. This time Lisbeth Salander

takes center stage in an investigation into three murders. Her personal history of abuse, neglect, and corruption is a horror story all its own, but her brilliant skill as a computer hacker and mathematical genius allows her insights into the puzzle posed, while her fearless integrity leads her to fight evil wherever she encounters it, however she must. Vance's deft pacing and inflection capture the character and mood of this menacing morality tale and allow Salander's voice to tell her own story. It speaks to Vance's skill at portraying this enigmatic character that listeners barely notice that she is voiced by a man.

Thriller; Mystery.

▶ **Parker, T. Jefferson**
L.A. Outlaws. **Charlie Hood Series.** Read by David Colacci and Susan Ericksen. 2008. Brilliance. ISBN: 9781423305989. 11 hrs.

Allison Murrieta, descendant of a 19th-century Mexican bandit, sees herself as a modern day Robin Hood, stealing from rich companies and giving to charities. All is going well until she is targeted by a professional hit man, clearly backed by someone in the police department. Rookie deputy Charlie Hood, sympathetically voiced by Colacci, encounters Allison, whose chapters are read by Ericksen, and becomes enamored—of her and her mission. Allison is quickly caught up in a situation far beyond her ken, and the good cop is barely equipped to help. Allison's chapters explore her complicated life as single mom, teacher, and philanthropist, but Ericksen also underlines the dark tone—we know this won't end well. Together the narrators present a gripping thriller, both suspenseful and inspiring, that offers action and characters with heart.

Thriller.

Herstory: Historical Fiction from a Female Perspective

Female characters voice a unique perspective on history written by women. These intimate accounts, both true and fictional, take listeners to other times and places, with events seen from a slightly different, and often very personal, point of view.

▶ **Allende, Isabel**
Inés of my Soul. Read by Blair Brown. 2006. Books on Tape. ISBN: 9781745936023. 12.5 hrs.

Inés Suárez, who accompanied the Spanish to Chile in the mid-16th century, dictates this fictional memoir. Allende's novel offers a stunning account of the founding and settling of a country, providing a slightly different take on the conquistador experience. Colorful descriptions illuminate characters and setting, but in addition to domestic issues, there are also battles and struggles, with good and bad characters among Indians and Spanish alike. Brown's husky voice and dignified narration capture the tone and character of Inés, as well as the lyrical language and musical cadence of the prose. Her slight Spanish lilt adds just the right note to this deftly woven mix of fascinating social, historical, and cultural details.

Historical Fiction; Women's Fiction; Literary Fiction.

Colin, Beatrice
The Glimmer Palace. Read by Justine Eyre. 2008. Books on Tape. ISBN: 9781415954904. 14.5 hrs.

Born in Berlin at the turn of the 20th century, Lilly Nelly Aphrodite faces both personal and national disasters in this lively look at Germany's turbulent history in the first half of the century. Surviving an orphanage and the shortages of her early years, Lilly triumphs and becomes an iconic film star, only to face personal misfortunes and a struggle to survive as the country's fortune falls. Eyre gives the young Lilly an air of innocence and vulnerability that matures into an intense and knowing voice. She smoothly navigates a range of other characters and accents in presenting the large, diverse cast. Eyre is at her best in reflecting Colin's passionate account of a woman caught up in history's flow, who is not always safe, as this bittersweet story reveals.

Historical Fiction; Women's Fiction; Literary Fiction.

Essex, Karen
Stealing Athena. Read by Susan Denaker. 2008. Books on Tape. ISBN: 9781415949009. 18.5 hrs.

Essex frames this fascinating tale with the history of the Elgin marbles, removed from the Parthenon in Athens in the early 19th century by Lord Elgin, then ambassador to Constantinople. On another level she explores the role of women in history. Denaker has clearly taken the task of voicing these complex women to heart. Initially we meet the lovely, adventurous, wealthy, and intelligent Mary Nisbet, voiced in a soft Scottish lilt. She marries Elgin and captivates the heads of state in Europe and the Middle East. In a distinctive and husky voice, Denaker next portrays the philosopher Aspasia, Pericles's mistress and an important influence at the time the marbles were carved by Pheidias. Aspasia and Nisbet suffer from double standards in both centuries, but Essex, aided by Denaker's skill in depicting these fully realized and sympathetic characters, demonstrates that, despite their lack of legal power, their influence was extensive. Individual voices for characters in both centuries keep listeners grounded, as we follow the lives of two fascinating women who were linked to more famous men.

Historical Fiction; Literary Fiction.

Gloss, Molly
The Hearts of Horses. Read by Renée Raudman. 2009. Tantor Media. ISBN: 9781400141968. 9.5 hrs.

Our sympathetic and engaging heroine Martha Lessen is a woman trying to find her place in the male world of broncobusting—or horse gentling, as she would have it—in rural Oregon in the winter of 1917, when able-bodied men are off at war. As she rides the "circle," working with the horses at the far-ranging homesteads, she introduces us to the diverse community of ranchers and farmers trying to hold on to their land and their dreams. Raudman voices this quiet, independent woman in a soft, deferential mezzo, and she gives each community member an appropriate voice, accent, and cadence. Rich in details and character, this novel reveals much about life on the home front, gentling horses, coping in a hardscrabble life, and making one's place. Raudman's reading underlines the leisurely pace of life in this rustic country, and her mindful narration enhances the effect of the lyrical prose in this heartwarming, homespun tale.

Historical Fiction; Women's Fiction; Western; Literary Fiction.

Stewart, Elinore Pruitt
Letters of a Woman Homesteader. Read by Kate Fleming. 2003. InAudio. ISBN: 1584724722. 5.25 hrs. Nonfiction.

The author's actual letters, written at her Wyoming ranch from 1909 to 1913, reveal much about daily life in the West and even more about the characters who settled there. Fleming clearly delights in the task of reading these letters, providing each of the personalities described with her own voice and offering a revealing, but not necessarily introspective, look at the author. Fleming's narration conveys the spirit of the kind of woman who could have survived here, widowed and on her own. Humor, accents, and cadence all reinforce this characterization and turn this account into a truly delightful and insightful glimpse of prairie life from one woman's perspective.

History.

Inside Their Heads: Psychological Suspense

One of the reasons we love novels of psychological suspense is that they take us inside the minds of the protagonists, often a scary place to be. Audio intensifies the feeling, whether we're caught with genuine madmen or simply with characters whose sanity might be questionable.

Abrahams, Peter
Oblivion. Read by Ken Marks. 2006. Recorded Books. ISBN: 9781428122789. 11.25 hrs.

Memory can play tricks on anyone, especially a man with a brain tumor who has just had a seizure; and after such brain trauma, memory sometimes simply disappears. Marks leads us step-by-step through private investigator (P.I.) Nick

Petrov's frustrating attempts to regain his memory in order to continue his last case, which involves a missing girl. Marks's narration underlines the compelling sense of urgency, as Petrov tries to fill in the blanks of the case and his life. But Petrov has gained something too: the ability to sense feelings behind actions and the mood and tone of encounters. This layered tale, which plays with memories and perceptions, offers the perfect stage for Marks to explore the nuances of character and our understanding of what really goes on in our minds.

Psychological Suspense; Literary Fiction.

Cook, Thomas H.

The Cloud of Unknowing. Read by Stephen Hoye. 2007. Tantor Audio. ISBN: 9781400104093. 8.5 hrs.

Cook keeps listeners off balance throughout this curiously structured investigation of a crime. When his sister's schizophrenic son dies in a drowning accident, David Sears is pulled into her attempts to prove her ex-husband actually murdered their son. The narration further unsettles listeners by alternating between a police detective's interview with David and David's own first-person account of his activities. Just what is his role? Hoye's matter-of-fact narration intensifies the moody creepiness of the story and the characters, as he makes us privy to David's thoughts and actions. Who is guilty? Who is sane? A haunting, shocking tale.

Psychological Suspense.

Goodman, Carol

The Lake of Dead Languages. Read by Vivienne Benesch. 2002. BBC Audiobooks America/Sound Library. ISBN: 079272836X. 13.75 hrs.

Jane Hudson returns to teach Latin at the isolated upstate New York private school where she once studied, but the tragedies from her past are being replicated in the present—in frighteningly similar ways. The haunting tales of crimes and passions past and present intertwine, and Jane and her young daughter are placed in jeopardy. Benesch's rich voice enhances the dark, evocative tone and emphasizes the sense of menace that drives the story. She carefully contrasts the voices of Jane as both student and teacher and skillfully communicates the psychological undertones that create the evocative mood.

Psychological Suspense.

Lindsay, Jeff

Darkly Dreaming Dexter. **Dexter Series.** Read by Nick Landrum. 2004. Recorded Books. ISBN: 1402596324. 8.5 hrs. ♼

Lindsay and Landrum take us inside the mind of a serial murderer in the madcap adventures of Dexter Morgan, splatter expert for the Miami Police Department and a serial murderer of serial murderers. Dexter's ominous "Dark Passenger" directs his vigilante activities, but otherwise, the amoral Dexter simply acts human, as best he can. Listeners can only sit back and imagine the action, related in grisly, chilling detail, as the amusing and oddly sympathetic Dexter satisfies his baser instincts while making the area safer by killing only the deserving. Landrum does such a good job with the range of characters that listeners may forget there is a single reader.

Psychological Suspense; Mystery.

▶ **Rendell, Ruth**
13 Steps Down. Read by Ric Jerrom. 2005. Sound Library/BBC Audiobooks America. ISBN: 0792737512. 11.25 hrs.

Rendell, who also writes as Barbara Vine, tells a chilling tale of murder and obsession, with ghosts (real or imagined) and dreams that invade reality. Michael "Mix" Cellini obsesses over Britain's famous Christie murder case and a fashion model, as his landlady, Gwendolyn Chawcer, confronts her own mental decline. Meanwhile, the house they live in decays symbolically around the two. Jerrom portrays the dissolution of both characters, from their early more lucid days to the tragic denouement. His dark voice captures the menacing atmosphere as he leads readers into these disturbed minds.

Psychological Suspense.

Just the Facts, Ma'am:
Police Detective Stories

The phrase "Just the Facts, Ma'am" may not resonate with the younger generation, but it does with those of us who first experienced *Dragnet* on radio or television. Police detective mysteries continue to thrill and chill listeners, providing details of crime fighting from the policeman's point of view. The titles listed are all parts of ongoing series. They are chosen as representative titles, not necessarily the first in each series.

Connelly, Michael
The Closers. **Harry Bosch Series.** Read by Len Cariou. 2005. Books on Tape. ISBN: 1415908192. 11.75 hrs.

After a brief retirement, Harry Bosch returns to the Los Angeles Police Department, assigned to "Open-Unsolved Case Squad," aka cold cases. DNA tests open up the 1988 shooting of a high school girl, but as he and partner Kiz Rider pursue clues, they're hampered by police politics past and present. Bosch's character continues to grow, and narrator Cariou adds a new spark of enthusiasm to the detective's gravelly voice and enlivens the full cast. An unhurried and thorough investigation, rich in psychological overtones, with intriguing characters and a complex, layered plot. Cariou navigates it all, and brings listeners along for the ride.

Mystery.

Crombie, Deborah
Water Like a Stone. **Duncan Kincaid and Gemma James Series.** Read by Michael
Deehy. 2007. BBC Audiobooks America. ISBN: 9780792738671. 14.5 hrs.

This 11th entry in the series starring Scotland Yard Chief Inspector Duncan
Kincaid and his life partner Detective Inspector Gemma James takes place in
Kincaid's hometown in Cheshire. Dangerous secrets lead to multiple interre-
lated cases, past and present, involving this vividly described small town and
life along the canals. Deehy manages the complex cases and multiple red herrings with ease, but series fans may be just as interested in the personal com-
plications, as Kincaid and James work through their relationship. His skill with
multiple accents—both from London and Cheshire—add to the authenticity of
the performance.
Mystery.

James, P. D.
The Murder Room. **Adam Dalgliesh Series.** Read by Charles Keating. 2004.
Books on Tape. ISBN: 0736696067. 13.5 hrs.

When a murder occurs at a small museum faced with foreclosure, Scotland
Yard's Commander Adam Dalgliesh is called in to investigate this complex puzzle involving family problems that just might lead to murder. Keating conveys
James's lyrical prose and haunting introspective tone, and his reading evokes the
inner lives of her detective and familiar series character. The large cast allows his
skill with accents and speech cadences to shine, as he personifies suspects and
police alike. A complex, layered mystery, rich in language and atmosphere.
Mystery.

▶ **Robinson, Peter**
Friend of the Devil. **Inspector Alan Banks Series.** Read by Simon Prebble. 2008.
Books on Tape. ISBN: 9781415948491. 13.5 hrs.

Separate cases investigated by Detective Chief Inspector Alan Banks and
his erstwhile partner and lover Annie Cabbot seem unrelated until a link to past
crimes throws both investigations and detectives together. Flawed but sympathetic and introspective characters, solid investigative techniques often hampered by office politics, and a dark mood lightened by the ubiquitous discussion
of pop tunes and jazz make this series an exemplar of British police procedurals.
Prebble's outstanding narration provides unique voices for all characters and
captures the undercurrents of their private lives. The dialog sings, and Prebble's
narration adds depth to a fine mystery.
Mystery; Crime Thriller.

Sandford, John
Broken Prey. **Prey Series.** Read by Richard Ferrone. 2005. Recorded Books.
ISBN: 1419340484. 11.75 hrs.

Gruesome descriptions of victims may make Sandford's popular series
tough to listen to, but the wonderful descriptions of the Minnesota landscape and

the appealingly complex hero, not to mention the labyrinthine plots, make this a winner. A serial murderer is at large, and Davenport, head of the Minnesota Bureau of Criminal Investigation, realizes early on that the person who seems responsible couldn't have planned this on his own. Who's running him—and how do they stop the real villain? Ferrone's sonorous baritone suits the ruminative Davenport perfectly, and he even pulls off lighter moments as the detective tries to fill his new iPod with the 100 best rock songs. Though a recent title in a long-running series, this is a good entry point for listeners who appreciate well-drawn characters, seamless investigations, and disturbing and atmospheric mysteries.
   Mystery; Crime Thriller.

From History to Myth: Legendary Heroes and Heroines

Bigger-than-life characters fill both fact and fiction. These stories explore the roots of their fame while enhancing their legends.

Allende, Isabel
Zorro. Read by Blair Brown. 2005. HarperAudio. ISBN: 006078959X. 15 hrs. Ⓨ🅐 📧
   Allende's interpretation of Zorro's early life makes for a sprawling saga, colorful and rich in family details and adventure. Brown's mesmerizing narration takes readers from Old California to Spain and back again, as we learn the source of Zorro's passion for justice and follow him and his companions on their escapades. A vividly described character piece set against an exotic backdrop filled with cultural, historical, and political details and familiar figures from history, including Pirate Jean LaFitte.
   Literary Fiction; Historical Fiction; Adventure; Coming-of-Age.

▶ Carey, Peter
True History of the Kelly Gang. Read by Gianfranco Negroponte. 2002. Recorded Books. ISBN: 9781402521072. 14.5 hrs. 🏆 Ⓨ🅐 📧
   Carey and Negroponte bring Ned Kelly, Australian Outback folk hero of the late 1800s, vividly to life in this fascinating tale. The novel's premise is that Kelly has written his autobiography as letters to the daughter he never met, and Negroponte's interpretation captures the energy and bigger-than-life persona, complete with his Australian accent and colorful slang. This mix of historical facts artfully embellished with psychological insights into a unique character enthralls listeners.
   Literary Fiction; Historical Fiction; Western.

Kolpan, Gerald
Etta. Read by Kirsten Potter. 2009. Blackstone Audio. ISBN: 9781433259302. 10 hrs.

Intrigued by the fact that so little is known about the Wild Bunch's Etta Place, Kolpan imagines a realistic biography from the scraps of history. Potter's elegant performance depicts both Etta's aristocratic roots and her flamboyant career as Harvey Girl, horsewoman and sharpshooter, and train robber, as well as the disparate cadences of the elite society of Philadelphia's Main Line and the speech of the outlaw band she joins. The Sundance Kid and Butch Cassidy figure prominently in a favorable light, while the representatives of the Pinkerton Agency don't fare as well. Etta's journal entries, newspaper articles, and Sundance's letters to his respectable father further enhance the authentic feel and underline the humor. A colorful, stylish historical romp.

Historical Fiction; Adventure; Women's Fiction.

Pressfield, Steven

The Virtues of War: A Novel of Alexander the Great. Read by John Lee. 2004. Books on Tape. ISBN: 1415913285. 12 hrs.

Pressfield sets up this account of the life of Alexander as a memoir, with the general on campaign telling his story to his brother-in-law. The approach offers a singularly intimate look at a complex man—a soldier and military tactician who relives battles won and lost and displays an acute intelligence of war and people. Lee's deep, gravelly voice makes him a popular narrator of historical epics. He demonstrates his talents here, as he makes Alexander into a full-blown and very sympathetic character driven by his daemon to strive onward, always battling in his quest to reach the eastern shore of the known world. The burden of the extensive descriptions of battles, weapons, and more might prove too much in the hands of a lesser narrator, but Lee's deft touch enlivens the authentic details while revealing an Alexander who lives up to his formidable reputation.

Historical Fiction; Military Fiction.

Scott, Manda

Dreaming the Eagle: A Novel of Boudica, the Warrior Queen. **Boudica Series.** Read by Josephine Bailey. 2003. Books on Tape. ISBN: 0736693343. 22.5 hrs.

This first title in Scott's trilogy introduces Britain's legendary Celtic queen and follows her from childhood to her early battles against the Romans in the first century. Bailey's lovely, bell-like voice perfectly captures the image-rich language and tone of this coming-of-age tale and adds a mystical aura. Adventure, battles, and betrayals share the stage with fascinating explications of Celtic rituals and beliefs.

Historical Fiction; Coming-of-Age; War Stories.

A Man's Got to Make a Living: Assassin Heroes and Antiheroes

It may be the character or the tone or the edgy story that attracts listeners. From deadly earnest to, well, earnest, these disturbing stories, seen through the eyes of an assassin, fulfill a desire to participate in dangerous deeds.

Cain, Tom
The Accident Man. Read by John Lee. 2008. Books on Tape. ISBN: 9781415947012. 12.25 hrs.

What happens when a contract killer develops a conscience? When hit man Samuel Carver discovers that his latest targets were not terrorists but Princess Diana and her lover, he sets out to find those responsible for setting him up. Lee's calculated pace and edgy intensity dramatize Carter's relentless search across Europe, as well as his determination to exact revenge. His rich, deep voice perfectly reflects this debut thriller's gritty, nightmare tone, as the flawed hero plots his bloody payback step-by-step.

Thriller.

Deaver, Jeffery
Garden of Beasts. Read by Jefferson Mays. 2004. Recorded Books. ISBN: 1419302213. 13.5 hrs. ♈

Paul Schumann, American hit man, arrives with the U.S. Olympic team in Berlin in 1936 with orders to kill members of Hitler's select cadre. If he is successful, the U.S. government has promised him a new start with past crimes forgiven. Trying to stay one step ahead of both the Berlin police and the Gestapo, Schumann traverses the streets of Berlin and the Olympic Village, facing danger and the possibility of discovery and betrayal at every step. Mays navigates accents and the diverse personalities with ease, presenting characters facing terrible moral dilemmas in a beautiful city where the undercurrent of evil is percolating upward. Building tension and a sharp sense of time and place add to this twisty tale of one man's mission. But is he hoping to serve justice or himself?

Thriller; Historical Fiction.

▶ **Eisler, Barry**
The Last Assassin. **John Rain Series.** Read by Michael McConnohie. 2006. Listen & Live Audio. ISBN: 9781593160807. 10 hrs.

The first-person thrillers in this series offer glimpses into the mind of a re-luctant assassin. Half-American, half-Japanese John Rain passes anonymously in both worlds, the perfect cover for his profession. In this excellent entry, which harkens back to the first and as yet unrecorded title, Rain finds his job has put his estranged wife and son in danger, and his concerns for their safety intensify his own peril as he tries to protect them from Japanese gangsters. McConnohie's bleak and melancholy tones skillfully convey the edgy character of this troubled loner, torn between obligation and an overwhelming desire to escape his role. His cadence captures speech patterns of the Japanese and Americans who fill the case, as he takes listeners on this exploration of the dark side of the Japanese soul. Enriched by a moody, nightmare tone, this character-driven series leaves no doubt about the downsides of this job.

Thriller.

Liss, David
The Ethical Assassin. Read by William Dufris. 2006. Brilliance. ISBN: 1423309294. 13 hrs.

Lest listeners imagine that assassins are all dark and dangerous, Liss offers Melford, an assassin in the midst of his latest mission, who is surprised by Lem, a naive young encyclopedia salesman. Dufris's exuberant reading exposes the absurdist bones of this romp, with over-the-top characterizations from the redneck police chief to the monumentally innocent Lem and the self-righteous polemic-spouting assassin. The story Dufris relates is no less absurd than the characters, and the violence flows as readily off his tongue as do the philosophical ramblings. Dufris conveys the dark humor of Liss's outlandish take on the character of an assassin, who is anguished by the impending political, philosophical, and moral ruin of Florida.

Literary Fiction; Humor.

Morgan, Richard K.
Thirteen. Read by Simon Vance. 2007. Tantor Media. ISBN: 9781400134311. 23 hrs.

Imagine a future world where a government experiment has gone awry and genetically engineered fighting machines, the eponymous Thirteens, have become so dangerous that they have been exiled to Mars. When one of the Thirteens escapes and wreaks havoc, Carl Marsalis, a Thirteen-turned bounty hunter/assassin, is hired to catch him. Vance deftly evokes the sensibility of a man created to kill who doesn't want to play that game anymore. He navigates the plot twists and violence, voices a disparate cast of characters, and draws listeners inexorably into the plight of this aggressive and unsocial warrior battling his own kind as well as corruption throughout his universe.

Science Fiction.

When Life Imitates Art: Audio Memoirs

As long as we remember that memoirs are based on memories of what happened, not necessarily the facts, we can sit back and enjoy these very personal glimpses into fascinating lives.

Clinton, Bill
My Life. Read by Bill Clinton. 2004. Random House. ISBN: 0739317067. 6.5 hrs. Abridged. Nonfiction. 🎧

Abridged from more than 50 hours to about 6.5, Clinton's award-winning recounting of the highs and lows of his life offers a comfortable, candid, and very intimate look at the former president. He doesn't shy away from the issues, including Monica Lewinsky, but he also offers insights gained from his political experiences and emphasizes his relationships with Hillary and Chelsea. Reading this himself allows Clinton to put his own inimitable verbal spin

on his personal story. (Interested listeners might also appreciate the unabridged version read by Michael Beck and published by Books on Tape.)
Memoir; Politics.

Didion, Joan
The Year of Magical Thinking. Read by Barbara Caruso. 2005. HighBridge Audio. ISBN: 159887005X. 5.25 hrs. Nonfiction. ♔ Ⓨ🄰 ☙
As poignant and moving as the book is—and this story of Didion's year after her husband's sudden death while she still had to care for her terminally ill daughter is that—Caruso's performance is even more so. Her simple, direct reading evokes the emotional depth of this heartfelt memoir, written as an act of mourning as well as a step toward the future. In Caruso's mesmerizing, melodious voice, listeners can hear both the pain and the smiles. Not to be missed.
Memoir; Grief.

Goodwin, Doris Kearns
Wait Till Next Year. Read by Suzanne Toren. 2004. Recorded Books. ISBN: 9781402587016. 8.25 hrs. Nonfiction.
Memoirs are known for offering surprises, and what could be more unexpected than an award-winning historian's memories of her youth in the 1950s as a Brooklyn Dodgers fan. While sharing books established her connection with her ill mother, baseball created the close bond she felt with her father. He taught her to keep score, and together they rehashed games. Details of turbulent Cold War days infiltrate this memoir, but baseball predominates, as she follows unsuccessful pennant races, the social unrest when Jackie Robinson joined the team, and finally, the end of an era with the Dodgers' departure for the West Coast. Toren's reading elevates the sense of personal connection and the role of memories in shaping lives. A wistful look back to an earlier time.
Memoir; Sports.

Grogan, John
Marley & Me: Life and Love with the World's Worst Dog. Read by Johnny Heller. 2006. Recorded Books. ISBN: 1419396307. 9.75 hrs. Nonfiction. ♔ Ⓨ🄰
It may be hard to tell whether this is the story of a man or of a dog, but in either case dog lovers will relish this upbeat chronicle of a dog and his would-be master. Aside from the confusion of whether the dog or the master is worse, Heller embodies Grogan and his attempts to instill manners into his loveable, but seemingly untrainable, dog. He conveys Grogan's great affection for his mischievous pet and employs heartwarming humor to dramatize the pains and pleasures of owning a dog. Despite a few tears, an upbeat mood fills every page of this tribute.
Memoir.

▶ Kimmel, Haven
A Girl Named Zippy: Growing Up Small in Moorland, Indiana. Read by Haven Kimmel. 2005. HighBridge Audio. ISBN: 1598870106. 6.5 hrs. Nonfiction.

Kimmel's memoir presents the best and worst of small-town life in the 1960s and 1970s: eccentric characters and not very much happening. But in this series of vignettes, Kimmel makes the most of her material, with folksy, humorous tales of life in a slower, gentler time. With clever prose, a deadpan delivery, and massive doses of the pleasures of childhood, Kimmel's comfortable, effortless delivery makes listening seem like sitting down with an old friend.

Memoir; Coming-of-Age.

Down These Mean Streets: Gregarious Gumshoes

In these urban mysteries, licensed investigators may have less authority than police but they also have more freedom to explore beyond the law. This subgenre started in the United States, and the examples listed here display the typical strong sense of place associated with these mysteries. Fans follow their favorite detectives from book to book in series that often span decades. Here are some representative titles.

Grafton, Sue

Q Is for Quarry. **Kinsey Millhone Series.** Read by Judy Kaye. Books on Tape. 2002. ISBN: 0736688366. 12 hrs. Ⓨ Ⓐ

Grafton sets her alphabet series starring P.I. Kinsey Millhone in fictional Santa Teresa, California, in the 1980s—before cell phones and computers were common. Kinsey was one of the first female P.I.s in a mostly male world, but she's as tough and stubborn as many of her male counterparts. Listeners can start almost anywhere in the series, as Grafton introduces Kinsey at the beginning of each, but this case, which harkens back to an unsolved 1969 murder, makes a good point of entry. In her investigation, the loner detective discovers something about her own roots. Kaye has continued to narrate series titles, and her warm and slightly gravelly voiced portrayal of Kinsey has created the persona listeners expect. Other characters get the same thoughtful treatment, creating a delight for the mind and the ears.

Mystery.

Lippman, Laura

Another Thing to Fall. **Tess Monaghan Series.** Read by Linda Emond. 2008. Recorded Books. ISBN: 9781428180642. 9 hrs.

This Baltimore-based series stars reporter-turned-investigator Tess Monaghan. When a film crew arrives in Baltimore, Tess is hired to protect one of the stars. However, another member of the crew is murdered, and Tess's bodyguard role transforms into investigator, complicated by the presence of Hollywood personalities. Emond's Baltimore accent adds another layer to listener's appreciation of this series, and the cast of movie figures, along with the dangerous villain, allow her to show off her skill. She makes us feel as if we're there, partnered with Tess in another suspenseful adventure.

Mystery.

Mosley, Walter

Little Scarlet. **Easy Rawlins Series.** Read by Michael Boatman. 2004. Books on Tape. ISBN: 1415902283. 7.5 hrs.

It's 1965 and although the worst of the Watts Riots are over, tempers still run high. When police discover the body of a black woman thought to have been murdered by a white man, they sensibly bring in unlicensed investigator Easy Rawlins to do the leg work in the black community. Boatman invests Rawlins with the heroic qualities that have made the series so popular. Rawlins is a thoughtful man of integrity caught between worlds, and Boatman's evocation of his speech patterns reflect his chameleon ability to speak the language his listeners expect. Boatman voices the spare yet sometimes lyrical prose with precision as he leads listeners through the serpentine plot, all the while revealing the historical moment through the eyes of a participant. Authentic details, an edgy mood, provocative issues, and textured social commentary often set P.I. mysteries apart, and this is an excellent example of the type.

Mystery.

Parker, Robert B.

Back Story. **Spenser Series.** Read by Joe Mantegna. 2003. Books on Tape. ISBN: 0736692797. 6 hrs.

No list of P.I.s would be complete without Parker's Spenser series, which set the standard for contemporary P.I.s. In addition to literate and snappy dialog filled with witty repartee, intriguing characters, and solid investigations, this Boston-based series pleases fans because of the details of the city and the personalities of its denizens. We can follow Spenser and sidekick Hawk down those mean streets into danger and out again. Mantegna excels at capturing the cadence of these dialog-rich mysteries. Each voice is distinct and every line—and joke—resonates. Here, Spenser is called to investigate an unsolved murder from the 1960s, one both the FBI and the Mob want to stay unsolved.

Mystery.

▶ Rozan, S. J.

Winter and Night. **Lydia Chin and Bill Smith Series.** Read by William Dufris. 2005. BBC Audiobooks America. ISBN: 0792736710. 13 hrs. ♛

Mysteries often require as serious an investigation into the detective's past as into the mystery of the present. When his nephew is arrested in New York City and escapes from jail, P.I. Bill Smith and his partner Lydia Chin are determined to find him. The trail leads to a football-mad New Jersey town with dark secrets that evoke Smith's own nightmares. In addition to the series characters, Dufris portrays a large cast of supporting players and their moods—from swaggering and rebellious to foul-mouthed and cynical. Dufris illuminates the unexpectedly mean streets of tangled secrets in small-town New Jersey. Mystery.

Real People: Biographies Worth Listening To

For many nonfiction fans, biographies are the leisure reading of choice. Although audio versions lack the photographs and extras often included in their print counterparts, they allow skilled narrators to enliven fascinating characters and their accomplishments.

Halberstam, David
The Teammates: A Portrait of Friendship. Read by Tate Donovan. 2003. Hyperion Audio. ISBN: 1401397492. 6 hrs. Nonfiction

As is typical for Halberstam's books, this is more than a biography of popular sports figures; it's a popular history of the sport, the times, and the players who had an impact on both. While Ted Williams may be the most famous of these Boston Red Sox players, he's not the sole focus. Dom DiMaggio, Johnny Pesky, and Bobby Doerr get equal space in this paean to some of the men who made baseball America's pastime. Narrator Donovan disappears into these stories, so that listeners are submerged in these nostalgic tales of men, friendship, and sports and are able to gain a better sense of why athletics matter.
Biography; Sports.

Herrera, Hayden
Frida: A Biography of Frida Kahlo. Read by Kimberly Schraf. 2002. Books on Tape. ISBN: 0736688013. 22.5 hrs. Nonfiction.

Herrera's portrait of Frida Kahlo follows her personal history as the flamboyant Mexican artist as well as a history of the times—the worlds of art, literature, and the rich and famous. Schraf's passionate portrayal captures the strength and vitality of a woman who overcame polio and a near-deadly accident, which left her in constant pain, to become one of the 20th century's greatest artists. Schraf's rich voice matches the opulent setting and sensuous story in this carefully documented biography.
Biography; Art.

McCullough, David
Truman. Read by Nelson Runger. 2004. Recorded Books. ISBN: 9781402578816. 54.75 hrs. Nonfiction. 🏆 YA 📚

Historian, scholar, and storyteller McCullough writes even-handed, insightful biographies of important American historical figures. Truman, one of our most unassuming presidents, becomes a figure to be reckoned with under McCullough's

pen. He is, after all, the president who saw the United States through the momentous events of the end of World War II and into the postwar years. Runger takes
us from Truman's boyhood in Missouri to the White House and to his retirement
with wife Bess. He conveys the author's affection for his subject as well as the
sense of Truman's character and his determination to remain a common man.
Biography; History.

▶ **Roberts, Cokie**
Founding Mothers: The Women Who Raised Our Nation. Read by Cokie Roberts.
2004. Harper Audio. ISBN: 0060527870. 6 hrs. Nonfiction

Roberts is one of the few authors skilled enough to narrate her own books,
and her pleasure in these richly detailed anecdotes is palpable. She brings her
considerable research—this is as much history and social history as biography—to recreate the lives of the women behind the men who founded our country. Roberts effortlessly demonstrates the importance of women in Colonial and
early U.S. society with no small measure of wit. Her conversational tone—it
often feels as if she's simply chatting with listeners—enlivens the stories of the
famous (Abigail Adams and Martha Washington) and those less well-known
(Eliza Pinckney and Deborah Read Franklin).
Biography; History; Social History.

Spoto, Daniel
Enchantment: The Life of Audrey Hepburn. Read by Kimberly Farr. 2006. Books
on Tape. ISBN: 9781415933640. 11.75 hrs. Nonfiction.

Hepburn's life was as varied, exciting, and memorable as the movies for
which she is best known. Spoto documents her childhood during World War II,
including her involvement with the Dutch Resistance, her Hollywood years, and
her post-film star life as a humanitarian and ambassador for UNICEF. Farr's
low-key narration suits Hepburn's character perfectly. Her affectionate, admir-
ing tone encourages listeners to take notice of this exceptional life.
Biography.

Real People in Fictional Worlds

Fictionalized stories of real people are almost as popular as biographies and
memoirs. Listeners look for a sense of what the characters were like based on
historical information, but the fictional setting allows for liberties that nonfiction writers do not enjoy.

Alexander, Robert
Rasputin's Daughter. Read by Josephine Bailey with Simon Vance. 2006. Tantor
Media. ISBN: 1400101948. 8.5 hrs.

Despite the title—and the fact that Rasputin's 18-year-old daughter Maria
does serve as the narrator—this fascinating and well-researched novel actually

recounts the last week of the notorious Grigori Rasputin's life. Bailey's perceptive reading makes this story very personal, and her skill with Russian names and words brings listeners right into the action. While the novel may clear up questions surrounding Rasputin's death, it also makes him an even more enigmatic figure, both saint and sinner. Vance sporadically voices one of the assassins, and both readers splendidly recreate the edgy mood in St. Petersburg in December 1916.

Historical Fiction; Biographical Novels.

▶ **Harris, Robert**
Imperium: A Novel of Ancient Rome. **Cicero Series.** Read by Simon Jones. 2006. Recorded Books. ISBN: 9781428135628. 13.5 hrs. Y A

Who would have thought Cicero could be so entertaining? Harris presents the great Roman orator's life as told by his confidential secretary (and the inventor of shorthand) Tiro. The novel is filled with familiar faces from history and Latin classes, fascinating details of Roman life and culture, and a wealth of political corruption and intrigue. Jones employs a confidential tone, rich in sly humor and wit, that pulls listeners into the tale. Latin rolls off his tongue as if he were born speaking it, and his performance brings Cicero to our rapt attention in this witty, sophisticated tale.

Historical Fiction; Literary Fiction; Biographical Novels.

Horan, Nancy
Loving Frank. Read by Joyce Bean. 2007. Brilliance. ISBN: 9781423332879. 15 hrs. ♛

As gossipy as any celebrity biography, this blend of fact and fiction explores the affair between world-renowned architect Frank Lloyd Wright and Mamah Borthwick Cheney. Told from Cheney's point of view, the story offers insight into her reflections and her side of the relationship as well as into Wright's character. Lurid details, along with particulars of architectural history and the fight for women's rights, are offered in polished language. Bean's elegant narration emphasizes our role as observers of the relationship, the events, and the emotions. Her graceful reading leads us through this sometimes melodramatic tale to its tragic conclusion.

Literary Fiction; Historical Fiction; Biographical Novels.

King, Susan Fraser
Lady Macbeth. Read by Wanda McCaddon. 2008. Tantor Media. ISBN: 9781400136155. 11.5 hrs.

Finally, the termagant of Shakespeare's tragedy takes this opportunity to tell her own fascinating story. Lady Gruadh, descended from kings, sees herself as a Celtic warrior and trains for battle, making her an excellent consort for King Mac Bethad, as they fight the nefarious King Duncan and his son Malcolm. McCaddon's lovely Scottish accents reflect the hearts and souls of her characters. There's an edge to McCaddon's young Gruadh, since she was never a sweet young thing, and as the lady matures, McCaddon adds a note of forthright as-surance. Each character receives a distinctive voice, and complex and unfamiliar Scottish names and terms permeate the atmosphere. Authentic historical details add to this dramatic, emotionally charged tale of love and ambition.

Historical Fiction; Women's Fiction.

Littell, Robert

The Stalin Epigram. Read by John Lee and Anne Flosnik. 2009. Tantor Media. ISBN: 9781400141548. 10.5 hrs.

Littell's elegant tribute to Russian poet Osip Mandelstam offers a fascinat-ing view of pre–World War II Russian life among artists and politicians, with glimpses of Pasternak, Gorki, and, especially, Stalin. Mandelstam's life is re-lated in first-person accounts by the poet, his wife and fellow poet, and others, from his notoriety as an anti-Stalinist to his confinement in a Siberian prison camp to the bleak years afterward. Lee's deep and sonorous voice perfectly matches the dark mood, and both he and Flosnik invigorate this chilling story of political repression with their intimate recounting of events. Authentic details fill the story, which reminds us of the names of the famous and not-so-famous Russians who suffered under Stalin's ruthless regime. This excellently read audio version makes the dense prose readily understandable, and potentially unpro-nounceable names roll off Lee and Flosnik's tongues with ease.

Historical Fiction; Literary Fiction; Biographical Novels.

Uneasy Lies the Crown: Stories about Royalty

There's royalty and then there's royalty. Novelists love to play with these ultimate rich-and-famous characters, sometimes presenting well-researched por-traits, at other times tweaking them just a bit.

Bennett, Alan

The Uncommon Reader. Read by Alan Bennett. 2007. BBC Audiobooks America. ISBN: 9780792750284. 7.75 hrs.

Imagine England's very proper queen walking her corgis and coming upon a mobile library parked at the palace gates for the benefit of the staff. It seems only polite to borrow a book. And thus Queen Elizabeth is transformed by the power of books and their stories. Bennett reads with an oh-so-proper upper-class British accent, as he recounts the royal obsession with books as a way to discover the outside world and learn about other people. Ironic humor, a playful tone, and even a surprise twist at the end make this an enjoyable—and quick—listen.

Literary Fiction; Gentle Reads; Humor.

Helprin, Mark
Freddy and Fredericka. Read by Robert Ian Mackenzie. 2005. Recorded Books. ISBN: 141934496X. 25.5 hrs.

Some novelists treat the monarchy seriously; others poke serious fun. The latter is the case here as Helprin drops the heir to the throne and his wife (thinly disguised caricatures of Prince Charles and Princess Diana) in New Jersey. Their mission: to bring America back into the fold, aka the British Empire. Enter our narrator who clearly enjoys the challenge of articulating a wide range characters and accents as much as listeners enjoy listening to him do it. To his Scottish brogue he adds a cacophony of accents representing the denizens of the Commonwealth, each distinctive and memorable. He comfortably carries the listener through the verbal acrobatics of endless puns and malapropisms, never neglecting the flamboyant parody of customs and characters on both sides of the Atlantic. A whimsical and hilarious send-up.

Literary Fiction; Humor.

Iggulden, Conn
Genghis: Birth of an Empire. **Conqueror Series.** Read by Stefan Rudnicki. 2007. Blackstone Audio. ISBN: 9781433215308. 15 hrs. [Y][A]

Not all royalty is crowned; some earn their titles and legion of followers as soldiers in the field. Rudnicki traces Genghis Khan, from his birth on the Mongolian steppes to his rise to fame in this first of Iggulden's excellent historical adventure trilogy. (Later volumes are published by Recorded Books and read by Richard Ferrone.) Rudnicki's deep bass voice has just the right edge to help establish readers in an unfamiliar time and place and set the tone for this sometimes violent but always engrossing story. Unusual names flow easily, and his sense of cadence gives one the feel of men riding horses, flowing over the worlds they conquer.

Historical Fiction; Adventure; Military Fiction; Biographical Novels.

▶ **Min, Anchee**
Empress Orchid. Read by Alexandra O'Karma. 2004. Recorded Books. ISBN: 1402574975. 18 hrs. [Y][A] 🐚

While some are born to royalty, others gain their crowns by cleverness and luck. Min's carefully researched portrait of Cix, the Empress Orchid, reveals a life at odds with that presented by the Communist regime. O'Karma's reading offers a wondrously rich portrait of a poor relation who becomes the emperor's concubine, then the mother of the last emperor, and regent and ruler of China at the end of the 19th century. Her reading maximizes the impact of the lyrical language and detailed descriptions of life inside and outside the Forbidden City, and provides a glimpse into the character of this politically astute and cultured monarch. O'Karma also narrates the sequel, *The Last Empress.*

Biographical Novels; Historical Fiction; Women's Fiction.

Naslund, Sena Jeter
Abundance: A Novel of Marie Antoinette. Read by Susanna Burney. 2006. BBC Audiobooks America. ISBN: 9780792745174. 18.5 hrs. 🏆

This intimate, fictionalized biography of the popular French queen takes the young "Toinette" from the safety of the Austrian court to the dangers of the French court, from a girl to a sophisticated manipulator of people and politics. Burney dispenses with accents and focuses on character, differentiating among the large cast through timbre and pitch. Her portrayal of Marie Antoinette reveals the character of the queen beyond her extravagances and shows her as a thoughtful caring wife, mother, friend, and philanthropist. A bittersweet but ultimately tragic portrait, enhanced by lush descriptions and a wealth of social, cultural and historical details.

Biographical Novels; Historical Fiction; Women's Fiction.

Second Bananas: Sidekicks

Long-running series with charismatic detectives and their sidekicks dominate the mystery, suspense, and thriller genres, and some of the most interesting series entries tell the stories of the second bananas. In audio versions these tales of the sidekicks allow narrators an opportunity to display their skills, because these characters provide an interesting contrast to the heroes.

Crais, Robert
The Watchman. **Elvis Cole and Joe Pike Series.** Read by James Daniels. 2007. Brilliance. ISBN: 9781593550424. 9 hrs.

This is the taciturn Pike's story, with series lead Elvis Cole providing comic relief. Through the complex, twisted plot, we discover much of Pike's past as a Marine, former Los Angeles policeman, and mercenary, before providing the muscle for Cole. Hired to keep a federal witness (a troubled heiress who saw something she shouldn't have) under cover and safe, Pike hires Cole to discover who wants her dead—and why. Daniels leaves listeners breathless, as the story races from one dangerous encounter to the next at a breakneck pace. He skillfully projects the story's emotional depth and combines the gritty details with an almost heartwarming tone. Daniels also gets full marks for his spot-on Valley Girl voicing of Larkin Barkley, a young woman who ultimately benefits from Pike's skill and life lessons.

Mystery; Thriller.

George, Elizabeth
Deception on His Mind. **Thomas Lynley Series.** Read by Donada Peters. 2005. Books on Tape. ISBN: 9781844561209. 22.8 hrs.

Sergeant Barbara Havers, for once without New Scotland Yard's aristocratic Thomas Lynley, finally gets her own case in this ninth entry in the series. Recovering from an injury, she follows her Pakistani neighbor and his daughter to the coast for a vacation and gets pulled into a racially charged murder investigation. Peters's pleasing voice easily handles the range of accents and classes, as well as George's lyrical prose. The interpretation of the sometimes tough-talking

Havers offers more than a glimpse into her softer side, while Peters's voice clearly reflects Havers's working-class origins.

Mystery.

Grimes, Martha

The Lamorna Wink. **Richard Jury Series.** Read by Donada Peters. 2000. Books on Tape. ISBN: 0736652078. 10.5 hrs.

While Scotland Yard's Richard Jury is following up on a case in Northern Ireland, his friend and sometimes fellow-investigator Melrose Plant (who has disdained the title Lord Ardry) escapes to Cornwall to relax—and perhaps escape his annoying Aunt Agatha. He leases a beautiful seaside home and discovers the tragic story of two children drowned there four years earlier. The disappearance of one woman and the murder of another put Plant right in the middle of the investigation, along with Jury's pal Brian Macalvie of the Devon and Cornwall police. Humor abounds, and its impact is intensified in Peters's excellent performance, but this mystery isn't concerned only with laughs. It also explores Plant's past and is filled with memories of his family and childhood. Peters heightens the emotional level in this humorous but bittersweet tale—justice is done but lives are lost—which adds another dimension to the series.

Mystery.

▶ Grippando, James

Last Call. **Jack Swyteck Series.** Read by Jonathan Davis. 2008. Recorded Books. ISBN: 9781428198210. 10.5 hrs.

Unjustly accused Theo Knight was rescued from death row by young lawyer Jack Swyteck, and the two have been friends ever since, with Theo often providing the muscle in Jack's investigations. This time the case is closer to home—the victim in the 20-year-old crime was Theo's mother, and Theo is determined to uncover the secrets from his own past. Davis fluently portrays the suspenseful yet bittersweet tone, the sympathetic characters (including Theo's Uncle Cy, a jazz musician with his own past), the smart and colorful dialog, and the growing sense of menace leading to inevitable violence. His smooth voice parallels the rich jazz theme, as he creates a community of distinctive voices in this suspenseful tale.

Thriller; Mystery.

White, Stephen W.

The Siege. **Alan Gregory Series.** Read by Dick Hill. 2009. Brilliance Audio. ISBN: 9781423390343. 14.75 hrs.

Sam Purdy, the policeman who lends a hand in psychologist Alan Gregory's myriad cases, has been suspended from the Boulder Police Department and finds himself in New Haven, where he is caught up in a nightmare terrorist attack at Yale University. Top students are held hostage in this complex and cinematic thriller that barrels along at a breakneck pace. Purdy joins maverick FBI investigators, and together, with a cameo by Gregory, they resolve the case. Hill maintains the relentless pace as the characters work against the clock to free the students. His meticulous reading also underlines the dark tone generated by the terrible randomness of violence. As in others in Gregory's series, there is more about character and psychology here than action, but the building tension drives the story, and Hill—and White—never loosen their grip on our attention.

Thriller; Mystery; Suspense.

Don't You Believe Them!: Unreliable Narrators

Listeners and readers have learned to trust the narrator. He directs the story and keeps us focused and on track. With this group, however, we should think twice before trusting the narrator, as each skillfully forces us to change our perceptions. All is not what it seems.

Christie, Agatha

The Murder of Roger Ackroyd. **Hercule Poirot Series.** Read by Robin Bailey. 2001. BBC Audiobooks America. ISBN: 9780792752745. 7 hrs. Y A

Fans of Christie's timeless puzzles smile at the mention of this one—not the title to start readers new to the author or genre! Dr. James Sheppard narrates this twisted tale, assists the inimitable Hercule Poirot, and explores and explains the multiple suspects and their motives. Bailey gives the doctor an affable, confiding air that makes us confidantes and draws us into this richly imagined mystery that highlights Christie's wit and meticulous plotting.

Mystery; Classic.

▶ Lehane, Dennis

Shutter Island. Read by Tom Stechschulte. 2003. Recorded Books. ISBN: 9781402556180. 9.5 hrs.

U.S. Marshalls Teddy Daniels and Chuck Aule arrive on this isolated offshore island, which houses a hospital for the criminally insane, to search for an escaped patient. It is summer 1954, and when a hurricane hits the island, Aule disappears. Teddy is left alone to face his growing fear that he may become a victim of whatever evil is being perpetrated there. Stechschulte takes listeners into the minds of the characters, making us privy to their doubts and fears and a partner in their futures. Nothing is what it seems, and while Stechschulte guides us through the switching perspectives, he also makes us intimate with violence. But nothing can prepare us for the final twist.

Psychological Suspense; Mystery.

Pears, Iain

The Portrait. Read by Simon Vance. 2005. Books on Tape. ISBN: 1415917876. 5.5 hrs.

Vance holds listeners enthralled with his haunting performance of a famous Scottish portrait painter recounting his past to his latest subject, the critic who first promoted and then panned him. A sense of foreboding hangs over the scene as we follow artist McAlpine's monologue. Just how mad is he? Can we trust his memories and his insidious plan for revenge? This chilling character study leaves listeners breathless, so convincing is Vance's creation of the sense of menace and perfidious charm.

Literary Fiction; Psychological Suspense.

Simmons, Dan

Drood. Read by John Lee. 2009. Books on Tape. ISBN: 9781415960738. 30 hrs.

Why wouldn't we trust Wilkie Collins, Dickens's fellow writer and good friend, and his account of Dickens's encounter with the mysterious Edwin Drood, a meeting that leads to his unfinished novel, *The Mystery of Edwin Drood*? Friend he may be, but a jealous one at best, and his drug-addled imaginings lead to a dangerous journey through London's underworld in search of the mysterious Drood, supposed master of Egyptian black arts. Lee carefully builds and sustains the unsettling atmosphere in this often melodramatic tale, as he gives voice to the increasingly disturbed characters and the growing menace. Listeners sense the dissolution of Collins's mind in his mental and physical meanderings through a dark and perilous London.

Literary Fiction; Historical Fiction; Biographical Novels; Horror.

Waters, Sarah

The Little Stranger. Read by Simon Vance. 2009. Books on Tape. ISBN: 9781415965115. 16 hrs.

As in the best gothics and more civilized 19th-century horror, something is haunting Hundreds Hall, home of the Ayers family, who, in this immediately post–World War II Britain, are a family in decline. Vance captures the moody, atmospheric tone and builds the chilling sense of menace, drawing listeners inexorably into this psychological tale. Is there really an evil presence, or are the servants merely suggestible? Might the ghost of the eldest child be responsible for the mysterious happenings? Listeners hear reports from the servants and the family, as well as from villagers in this gossipy small town, but all is filtered through the perceptions and understanding of Dr. Faraday in this first-person narrative. Eventually we listeners begin to wonder whether our trusted narrator may be more than simply an observer of these sinister, sometimes deadly, events.

Horror; Literary Fiction.

Up Close and Personal:
First-Person Accounts

Audio often provides a more intimate look into characters and their lives, but when the story is told in the first person, the connection between narrator, character, and listener is even more intense. Interestingly, listeners often have strong feelings about first-person novels—they love them or hate them.

Diamant, Anita
Day after Night. Read by Dagmara Dominczyk. 2009. Recorded Books. ISBN: 9781440750236. 8 hrs.

Four women, all Jewish survivors of the Holocaust, recall their pasts while held in a British detention camp in Palestine in 1945. Haunted by terrible memories, the young women flounder in the camp, which is in some ways little better than those of the Nazis. Dominczyk's emotional narration provides authentic voices for the women in Polish, Dutch, Parisian, and German accents, as well as to the large cast of British and Israeli characters. A poignant and inspirational tale of damaged characters who find ways to overcome their losses and move on.

Historical Fiction; Women's Fiction; War Stories.

Hosseini, Khaled
The Kite Runner. Read by Khaled Hosseini. 2004. Recorded Books. ISBN: 1402596650. 12 hrs. 🏆 ⓎⒶ 📖

Listeners either love or hate the author's reading of this dramatic character study of two Afghani boys divided by class in their war torn country. While Hosseini lacks the skills of a professional narrator, he brings genuine emotions to this very personal story, and his ability to evoke the characters, customs, land, and language cannot be denied. Graceful, lyrical writing makes the gritty politics and tough themes of guilt and redemption stand out even more starkly in this candid first-person account.

Literary Fiction; War Stories.

Maron, Margaret
Slow Dollar. **Deborah Knott Series.** Read by C. J. Critt. Recorded Books. 2002. ISBN: 9781402570414. 8.75 hrs.

Many mystery series are told in the first person, as it intimately ties listeners to characters. Maron makes good use of this connection, offering her protagonist's thoughts and even inner battles, as her conscience, represented by The Preacher and The Pragmatist, wars throughout. While the first in the series, *The Bootlegger's Daughter*, stands as the best introduction to the series, this title, which features heroine Deborah Knott's extended family and a murder at a carnival, is another good entry point. Series narrator Critt excels at the regional accents as well as carnival jargon. Familiar characters, each identifiable by slight shadings in her voice, remind listeners of the pleasures of a good mystery in a long-running series.

Mystery.

Remarque, Erich Maria
All Quiet on the Western Front. Read by Frank Muller. 1994. Recorded Books. ISBN: 9780788734410. 7 hrs. ⓎⒶ 📖

Paul Baumer, a young German, relates the enthusiasm with which he and his classmates enter the war, but their coming-of-age at the front simply leads to death. Authentic and tragic, this insider's view of World War I offers sympathetic characters, gritty details of life at the front, and a moving picture of the hopelessness wrought by the devastating horrors of war. Muller's straightforward delivery of this classic antiwar novel heightens its impact and underlines its emotional depth. A mesmerizing reading of a quintessential tale.

Literary Fiction; Classic; War Stories; Coming-of-Age.

▶ **Robinson, Marilynne**

Gilead. Read by Tim Jerome. 2005. BBC Audiobooks America. ISBN: 0792734343. 9 hrs. ♔ ☙

Rev. John Ames is dying, and since he knows his young son will never remember him, he leaves behind a journal. Filled with self-deprecating humor and honest advice, this touching family history documents the young man's legacy and offers instructions to guide his journey into manhood. With his melodious bass voice and midwestern accents, Jerome inhabits the character. His perceptive reading offers another layer to listener's appreciation of this novel, as he pulls us into character and story, exposing the emotional core of the man behind these thoughtful ruminations and offering a glimpse into a dying man's life.

Literary Fiction; Historical Fiction.

By Women, for Women:
Women's Lives and Relationships

Female readers and listeners alike flock to the stories written by and about women.

Cleage, Pearl

I Wish I Had a Red Dress. Read by Caroline Clay. 2002. Recorded Books. ISBN: 9781402540301. 8.75 hrs. ♔

Cleage's distinctive rhythms and lush, image-rich prose are meant to be heard, and Clay portrays the characters and their stories to perfection. Widowed social worker Joyce Mitchell has a satisfying life helping troubled young women restart their own lives, but she longs for one more opportunity to wear that red dress that signifies freedom for her. Authentic characters and dialog, a solid sense of place on Lake Michigan, and a heartwarming story of the solidarity and power of women working together resonate in Clay's intelligent and heartwarming performance.

Women's Fiction; Multicultural Fiction.

Dallas, Sandra

Prayers for Sale. Read by Maggi-Meg Reed. 2009. BBC Audiobooks America. ISBN: 9780792760108. 9 hrs.

Reed's haunting, gravel-voiced rendition of the memories of Hennie Comfort provide glimpses into the history of a Colorado mining town and Hennie's colorful past. No longer able to live on her own in these rustic surroundings, Hennie is preparing to move back east to live with her daughter. However, when Nit Spindel, whom Reed evokes with a fluting young voice, moves to town with her miner husband, Hennie finds a receptacle for her stories at last. Homespun truths and timeless tales of secrets, loss, and redemption epitomize universal themes. The power of stories resonates in Reed's inspiring reading.

Historical Fiction; Women's Fiction.

▶ **Trigiani, Adriani**

Lucia, Lucia. Read by Cassandra Campbell. 2003. Books on Tape. ISBN: 0736693831. 10.5 hrs.

Greenwich Village may not be rural Virginia, the setting of Trigiani's popular Big Stone Gap series, but the families here are just as close-knit and demanding. Budding playwright Kit reluctantly accepts an offer of tea from her neighbor, only to find herself enchanted by Lucia's stories of life in this Italian neighborhood during the 1950s. An independent woman who worked as a custom seamstress for a prestigious department store, Lucia took advantage of the post–World War II social changes that opened many doors to women. Tales of the rich and famous of New York society hold Kit's attention and ours in this copiously detailed and ultimately feel-good story of women and families and responsibilities. Campbell moves easily among the characters, voicing the energetic young playwright and the endearing older woman with equal parts humor and charm, making the most of Trigiani's sparkling dialog and storytelling.

Women's Fiction; Gentle Reads; Historical Fiction.

Valdes-Rodrigues, Alisa

The Dirty Girls Social Club. **Dirty Girls Social Club Series.** Read by Isabel Keating. 2003. BBC Audiobooks America. ISBN: 0792728939. 12 hrs.

In this first of a series, we meet six upwardly mobile Latina friends, all graduates of Boston University, and learn their stories and their dreams. Each one, complex, flawed, and with a secret weakness, tells her own often irreverent story as their lives continue to intertwine. Keating creates fresh, young voices for each woman, and her unmistakable appreciation for and enjoyment in their lives translates effectively to listeners as well. Bawdy humor and generous affection fill this novel.

Women's Fiction; Humor.

Weiner, Jennifer

In Her Shoes. Read by Barbara McCulloh. 2003. Recorded Books. ISBN: 1419308963. 15.75 hrs.

In all her novels of women and their lives, Weiner blends serious issues with humor as she explores her characters' predicaments. Here, two sisters, one a stuffy lawyer and the other a lovely lush, are forced to develop a real relationship for the first time in their lives. McCulloh reads with intelligence and confidence, giving voice to the young women's characters and plights as they discover and accept more about themselves and each other. She projects the sweetness of their relationship and the joys—and difficulties—of being family.

Women's Fiction; Humor.

Chapter Five

Setting

Setting adds an extra dimension to books. In audiobooks, narrators aid the writer in transporting listeners into the story's locale. Setting can be closely linked to language in audio versions, as books set in a particular location may require a specific accent or speech pattern for authenticity. If the accents don't ring true, narrators lose their audiences.

Setting also includes background details, that extra material that enhances story in both fiction and nonfiction. Incorporating these numerous details can take time and attention away from the characters and story, but the best narrators make these fascinating facts an integral part of the production by their engaging and enthusiastic reading. For example, skilled narrators describe maps and drawings so seamlessly that listeners never miss the actual figures.

These selections place readers in settings around the world as well as in imagined worlds and cover a range of fiction genres and nonfiction topics. There are likely favorite authors to be found here as well as new discoveries.

We Are So Not Amused: The Dark Side of Amusement Parks

Despite Disney's best efforts, amusement parks are not only sources of fun—they're also excellent settings for horror and disasters of every ilk. These audiobooks consider the darker side carnivals, circuses, and amusement parks.

▶ **Bradbury, Ray**
Something Wicked This Way Comes. Read by Paul Hecht. 1999. Recorded Books.
  ISBN: 0788746375. 8 hrs. [Y][A]
    An out-of-season carnival arrives in town bringing mysterious events and
  mortal danger to two young boys who encounter evil and must carefully tread
  the line between illusion and reality. Bradbury's lush prose is made to be heard,
  and Hecht's reading suits the language, characters, and especially mood to
  perfection. His rich baritone reflects the menace of the carnival and the specters
  of the freak show, while his characterization of the boys and their responses
  adds a haunting quality to the novel that makes the evil very real.
    Horror; Fantasy; Coming-of-Age; Classic.

Child, Lincoln
Utopia. Read by Scott Brick. 2002. Books on Tape. ISBN: 0736690646. 19.5 hrs.
    Imagine a popular futuristic theme park suddenly sabotaged, with popular
  rides turned into death traps. Brick is at his best in building suspense as well as
  in creating believable, sympathetic characters caught in a nightmare. Tension
  builds quickly—time stamps at the start of chapters remind us that our heroes
  are working against the clock—as the story unfolds in the course of a single
  day. Technological jargon, plot twists and surprises, likeable characters, and
  nonstop action make it almost impossible to stop listening.
    Thriller; Suspense.

Hiaasen, Carl
Native Tongue. Read by George Wilson. 2003. Recorded Books. ISBN:
  9781402561931. 16 hrs. ♔
    This early Hiaasen eco-thriller pits the Wildlife Rescue Corps against
  Francis X. Kingsbury, landscape developer and owner of The Amazing King-
  dom of Thrills. All is not as it should be in this paradise run by a Disney wanna-
  be who is really a mobster on the lam trying to scam the government out of
  funds for endangered species. With a labyrinthine plot richly populated by petty
  thieves, an ex-governor turned eccentric environmentalist, and an ex-reporter
  just trying to make a living, Hiaasen's madcap romp offers a cynical exposé of
  the destruction of Florida's natural beauty by developers and tourists. Wilson's
  laid-back narration works perfectly with this bizarre and often violent tale and
  underlines the black and very dry humor that drives the story.
    Crime Thriller; Humor.

Karp, Matthew
The Rabbit Factory. **Mike Lomax and Terry Briggs Series.** Read by Tom Stechschulte and James Jenner. 2006. Recorded Books. ISBN: 9781428106093.
  15 hrs.
    Is no one safe at Lamaar's Familyland? When the employee playing the
  trademark cartoon figure Rambunctious Rabbit is strangled and visitors and
  employees associated with the California theme park turn up dead, Los Ange-

les policemen Mike Lomax and Terry Biggs are called in to investigate, and hilarity ensues. Stechschulte voices both cops and assorted good guys, while Jenner adds just the right edge to the comic bad guys. Together they entertain listeners with a twisty plot, eccentric characters, and edgy humor combined with a lot of heart.

Mystery; Humor.

O'Nan, Stewart

The Circus Fire: A True Story of an American Tragedy. Read by Dick Hill. 2004. Brilliance Audio. MP-3 ISBN: 9781596004832. 11 hrs. Nonfiction.

It's not just in fiction that disaster comes to the circus. Sometimes the horrors are all too real, as in O'Nan's detailed investigative nonfiction report of the 1944 fire under the big top in Hartford, Connecticut. O'Nan combines human interest with circus lore, as he reports on the lives of victims and their families before and afterwards the disaster, along with historical details of the Barnum & Bailey and Ringling Brothers circuses. He provides an impressively full account of the cause of the fire, the efforts to contain it, and the aftermath of the tragedy that cost the community 167 lives. Hill offers a low-key reading of this gruesome event, so filled with horrific details that a dramatic reading would be too much. Yet he captures O'Nan's journalistic view of events, causes, and results and leads listeners through the morbidly fascinating details.

History.

Not in Kansas Anymore: Fabulous, Fantastic Worlds

What good is fiction if it can't take us away to worlds almost beyond our imagining? This selection covers places far away and some very close to home, seen in ways we've never thought of them before.

Bear, Greg

City at the End of Time. Read by Charles Leggett. 2008. BBC Audiobooks America. ISBN: 9780792754718. 21.75 hrs.

In this lavishly inventive world of stories within stories, three characters capable of transcending time and space come together to attempt to save knowledge and memory in a postapocalyptic future Seattle, threatened by the encroaching Chaos. Leggett helps listeners navigate the lyrical but dense prose and the convoluted, layered story line while exposing Bear's richly imagined world. He establishes the dark tone from the beginning and creates intriguing, believable characters from the bleak future and even bleaker far future in this novel, which plays out like an intense role-playing game, with characters faced with choices and decisions that can ultimately save—or doom—the world. As imaginative as it is provocative.

Science Fiction.

▶ **Gaiman, Neil**

Neverwhere. Read by Neil Gaiman. 2007. HarperAudio. ISBN: 9780061373879. 12.5 hrs. ⓎⒶ

Gaiman leads listeners to the richly imagined world of London Below, populated by monsters as well as princesses and a real Earl who reigns at the Earl's Court underground stop. Londoner Richard Mayhew is enticed to this underground world when he helps Door, one of those who "fell through the cracks" of society. She appears in the normal London above but leads him back down to help her discover why her family was killed. Few authors have the skill and stamina to read their own works effectively, but Gaiman's witty and warm voice is a pleasure to listen to. He hits just the right notes in portraying the wide ranging cast of characters, from menacing and diabolical villains to the appealing and engaging characters who assist Door in her magical quest.

Fantasy.

Hearn, Lian

Across the Nightingale Floor. **Tales of the Otori.** Read by Kevin Gray and Aiko Nakasone. 2002. HighBridge Audio. ISBN: 1565117115. 8.5 hrs. ⓎⒶ

Set against a backdrop of a feudal warlord society in a country like medieval Japan, this first in a fantasy trilogy introduces hero Takeo and heroine Kaeda, along with a wealth of warriors and assassins. Gray narrates Takeo's first-person chapters, while Nakasone provides the captive Kaeda's third-person story in alternating chapters. Both skilled narrators embody their characters and dramatically present thoughts, actions, and emotions. Takeo escapes the destruction of his village, is taken in by a warrior, and discovers his special powers. Against this richly detailed landscape, the fates of the two are inexorably linked. Battles, romantic adventure, and graceful prose characterize this story, its haunting mood enhanced by thoughtful narration.

Fantasy; Coming-of-Age; Adventure; Romance.

Scholes, Ken

Lamentation. **Psalms of Isaac Saga.** Read by Stefan Rudnicki, Scott Brick, William Dufris, and Maggi-Meg Reed. 2009. BBC Audiobooks America. ISBN: 9780792764311. 15 hrs. ♛

Each of the readers portrays a different character and perspective in this complicated story (the first in a projected five-volume series), combining an effective use of variations in tone and cadence. This epic saga begins with the destruction of the fabled city of Winwar, and with that, the loss of all the vast knowledge stored there. Political machinations, a mix of science (robots who remember all) and magic, an exotic setting, and a vast cast, each with secrets, makes this a compelling read. Multiple viewpoints and voices enhance the complexity of character and story.

Fantasy.

Stephenson, Neal

Anathem. Read by William Dufris, Oliver Wyman, Tavia Gilbert, and Neal Stephenson. 2009. BBC Audiobooks America. ISBN: 9781427205902. 34 hrs.

Stephenson's playful philosophical adventure, part science fiction, part historical fiction, requires attention, but the skilled cast of readers illuminates the well-drawn, intriguing characters as well as the layered, complex story line, making listening a pleasure. On a world similar to Earth, society is divided between the monastic intellectuals and the secular populace who live more ordinary lives. When disaster threatens on another world, a group of intellectuals is sent to prevent catastrophe. While Dufris carries most of the narrative, vocal cameos thread through the novel, and Stephenson himself introduces each chapter with a word and definition from the planet's abstruse vocabulary. In fact, Stephenson plays with language throughout the lengthy novel, and amusement and understanding are heightened in the hearing.

Science Fiction; Humor; Literary Fiction.

Like Being There:
Audio for the Armchair Traveler

Some books, fiction and nonfiction, evoke a setting so completely that they transport us there. As listeners we remain in the safety of our armchairs—or wherever we happen to be—and relax as we journey there as accidental tourists.

▶ **Bryson, Bill**

In a Sunburned Country. Read by Bill Bryson. 2004. Books on Tape. ISBN: 0736689753. 10 hrs. Nonfiction

Journalist Bryson has traveled around the world and reported on diverse places, mundane and unusual, and on the people who live there. His love of the eccentric is given full rein in this offering, as he explores Australia, the continent known for vast distances, enormous contrasts in landscape and culture, and more venomous creatures than anywhere else on Earth. Bryson proves a chatty travel guide, and humor, both understated and outrageous, plays a vital role in his recounting of historical and contemporary facts and points of interest.

Travel; Humor; History.

Bushnell, Candace

One Fifth Avenue. Read by Carrington MacDuffie. 2008. Books on Tape. ISBN: 9781415950296. 16.5 hrs.

Veteran narrator MacDuffie introduces listeners to the rich-and-famous residents of the eponymous apartment building, one of New York's most prestigious addresses, in this engaging, gossipy tale. This is the New York of those who have it all, as well as those who only pretend, and this charming comedy of manners reveals lives drawn together at the chic downtown address. MacDuffie reads this arch comedy with élan, playfully highlighting the schemes and secrets of the tenants, as well as the underlying domestic comedy. Sometimes flamboyant, sometimes more subdued, she captures Bushnell's droll comedy and spot-on satire to perfection and makes us part of the city and the lifestyle.

Women's Fiction; Humor.

Goldberg, Myla

Time's Magpie: A Walk in Prague. 2004. Read by Bernadette Dunne. Books on Tape. ISBN: 1415907773. 3 hrs. Nonfiction.

Goldberg's quirky guide to historical and contemporary Prague is so short that it gives just a taste of the pleasures of this glorious city. Yet Dunne's charming reading takes us there, to a city of beautiful historic buildings now interspersed with American fast food restaurants and recovering from the Soviet pall. You can almost feel the cobblestones and hear the city sounds, as well as pick up the humor that underlies the account and flourishes in the voice of our affable tour guide. A fascinating glimpse of Prague that provides a preview for travelers and a pleasant introduction for the rest of us.

Travel; Humor; History.

McKinney-Whetstone, Diane

Tempest Rising. Read by Susan Spain. 2002. Recorded Books. ISBN: 9781440710421. 9.75 hrs.

McKinney-Whetstone's novels explore generations of black families in Philadelphia in layered tales of individuals, communities, and issues. Spain's silky voice embodies each character in this provocative story of three sisters caught in the wave of social changes attending the passage of the 1964 Civil Rights Act. She capitalizes on the author's keen ear for dialog and captures the language of the street. Rich characterizations, heart-wrenching images, and lyrical writing evoke a real feel of time and place and make these tales of mid-1960s Philadelphia and its black neighborhoods memorable.

Women's Fiction; Multicultural Fiction.

Rutherfurd, Edward

New York: The Novel. Read by Mark Bramhall. 2009. Books on Tape. ISBN: 9781415962794. 37 hrs.

From New York's history as an Indian village taken over by Dutch settlers to 9/11 and beyond, Rutherfurd provides a panoramic view of the city and the people and events that shaped it and the country. This sprawling saga follows families, rich and poor, as their fortunes change and lives intertwine over the generations. We lose ourselves in the story, as Bramhall lets the characters speak for themselves as events unfold. He guides listeners through the fascinating history of the city, as seen through the eyes of the participants in events. A satisfying homage to a great city.

Historical Fiction; Family Saga.

Life's Rough Edges:
Hard Times

While some books may have pictures that document events, audiobooks must rely on the skill of the reader to convey the physical, emotional, and spiritual hardships faced by characters. In this collection of fiction and nonfiction, narrators portray the interaction of setting and characters to explore the human drama in the worst situations: how people deal with hard times.

Buck, Pearl

The Good Earth. **House of Earth Trilogy.** Read by Anthony Heald. 2007. Blackstone Audio. ISBN: 9781433204067. 10.5 hrs. ♈ [Y][A] ⬱

Industrious farmer Wang Lung creates a better life for his family in early 20th-century China, but he learns too late that riches alone don't end the hard times. The difficulties one faces when rich are simply different from those one faces when poor. Heald's splendid performance of this Pulitzer Prize–winning classic spotlights Buck's sublime prose and universal themes. He voices the large cast of characters with changes in tone and pace to indicate age, gender, and class, and his wonderfully expressive, animated reading creates distinct personalities for the main players. The poignancy of Heald's narration exposes the difficult truths that Wang Lung must face.

Literary Fiction; Classic.

Egan, Timothy

The Worst Hard Time: The Untold Story of Those Who Survived the Great American Dust Bowl. Read by Patrick Lawlor. 2006. Tantor Media. ISBN: 1400132207. 12 hrs. Nonfiction. ♈ [Y][A] ⬱

This nonfiction history of the Great Depression centered in the southern Great Plains focuses on the people affected by the weather disaster that created the dust bowl. Egan documents events and then explores their impact on those who survived at terrible cost. Lawlor embodies myriad individual characters and their plights, while detailing the rural setting of the high southern plains and speculating on the politics of farming and the over-plowing that was partly responsible for the damage. His dark tone and evocative rendition of events allow listeners to anticipate the impending disaster and experience the incredible dust storms and their devastating effects. This heartfelt oral history receives an effective oral presentation.

History; Weather.

Gruen, Sara
Water for Elephants. Read by David Ledoux and John Randolph Jones. Highbridge Audio. ISBN: 11.5 hrs. ♛ 🔲🔲 📖

Hard times are what you make of them, as Jacob Jankowski's life reveals. His parents' sudden deaths mean the end of his veterinary school studies in the early 1930s, but by chance, he jumps a train that just happens to be a circus train, and that changes everything. Two narrators relate this tale told in flashbacks: Ledoux as the young Jacob, and Jones as the more than 90-year-old codger in an assisted living facility. Each narrator captures the spirit of this very engaging character, and their voices, edged with emotion, enthusiasm, and sometimes heartbreak, lead listeners through Jankowski's life during the Great Depression.

Historical Fiction; Literary Fiction.

Leonard, Elmore
The Hot Kid. Read by Arliss Howard. 2005. Recorded Books. ISBN: 1419340565. 8.25 hrs.

The kid of the title, a young U.S. Marshall who hopes to make a name for himself by capturing the F.B.I.'s most wanted outlaws, could just as easily be about the outlaw he pursues, who is trying his darndest to be number one on that list. Or so it seems in Leonard's 1930s Oklahoma, where crime and apprehension are both running wild. Leonard recreates the world of Bonnie and Clyde and John Dillinger, when public interest showered acclaim on bad men and good guys alike. Howard makes the most of Leonard's distinctive cadence—written to be spoken—and letter-perfect characters in this cinematic tale of men seeking a better life in Oklahoma's dust bowl.

Historical Fiction; Crime Thriller.

▶ **O'Nan, Stewart**
Last Night at the Lobster. Read by Jonathan Davis. 2007. BBC Audiobooks America. ISBN: 9780792750451. 3.45 hrs. 📖

Filled with the mundane details of the last shift at a New Britain, Connecticut, Red Lobster restaurant, this surprisingly touching account resonates with its timeless story of a job—and a moment—lost. Davis leads listeners step-by-step through Manny DeLeon's last night as the conscientious manager, and it is perhaps the wealth of details that create such a poignant, melancholy tale of characters and their relationships. A timeless, intimate look at hard times for a very ordinary group of everymen.

Literary Fiction.

Past Transgressions: Historical Mysteries

Appealing to fans of both historical fiction and mysteries, these puzzles, set firmly in the past, elucidate time and place while satisfying fans of who-dun-its.

Akunin, Boris
The Winter Queen. **Erast Fandorin Series.** Read by Michael Kramer. 2003. Books on Tape. ISBN: 0736699007. 9 hrs.

This first in the series introduces rookie policeman Erast Fandorin, a bumbling but intuitive investigator in Czarist Russia. Sardonic humor and authentic historical, cultural, and social details of 19th-century Russia fill this and subsequent mysteries in the series. Here, Fandorin is assigned to a routine case, the suicide of a student from a wealthy family, but his unwanted persistence leads to the discovery of a far-reaching conspiracy. Kramer navigates the elaborate names and Russian pronunciations with ease and clearly enjoys the undercurrent of humor as he leads listeners through the convoluted tale.

Historical Mystery.

Davis, Lindsey
The Silver Pigs. **Marcus Didius Falco Series.** Read by Christian Rodska. 2005. BBC Audiobooks America. ISBN: 0792738152. 9 hrs.

The private investigator (P.I.) may be a 20th-century invention, but that doesn't stop authors from creating characters who operate as P.I.s and setting their investigations in the past. Marcus Didius Falco is an "informer" for Emperor Vespasian in Rome (and to the ends of the Roman Empire) in the first century C.E. This first title in the series takes listeners back to the beginning, when Falco solves a murder in a British silver mine and meets Helena Justina, who later becomes his wife. Series narrator Rodska's performance emphasizes the clever dialog, wisecracking humor, and strong characterizations, as he takes us back in time.

Historical Mystery; Humor.

Greenwood, Kerry
Cocaine Blues. **Phryne Fisher Series.** Read by Stephanie Daniel. 2006. Bolinda Audio. ISBN: 9781741635485. 6 hrs.

Flapper-era woman-of-the-world Phryne Fisher plays amateur detective in Australia and sometimes beyond in mysteries rich in historical detail. Her investigations reveal social problems, as she tackles smugglers, robbers, murderers, and more. This first case involves a cocaine ring and back-street abortions. Daniel's interpretation of Phyrne and crew is pure delight. She always gets the tone just right, whether it is in sophisticated banter or thoughtful discussions, and the Australian cadences are spot-on—as are the accents. Bolinda needs to get busy and make more of the series available!

Historical Mystery.

Perry, Anne
The Cater Street Hangman. **Thomas and Charlotte Pitt Series.** Read by Davina Porter. 2000. Clipper Audio/Recorded Books. ISBN: 9781436149488. 9.75 hrs.

In this first entry in Perry's long-running series, Inspector Thomas Pitt of Scotland Yard investigates the murder of Charlotte Ellison's sister in Victorian London. In the process, Charlotte begins her career as a "snoop" and assistant to Pitt, since she still has entree into the highest levels of society, despite her eventual marriage to a lowly policeman. Porter narrates several early titles in the series and always brings her skill with accents and her ability to project the emotional layers of the characters and stories. Perry is known for her discussion of social problems, but there's humor here as well, and Porter displays a genuine affection for this pair of investigators, which mirrors their own feelings.

Historical Mystery.

▶ **Peters, Elizabeth**

Crocodile on the Sandbank. **Amelia Peabody Series.** Read by Barbara Rosenblat. 2003. Recorded Books. ISBN: 9781402566875. 9 hrs.

Join Amelia Peabody, a Victorian gentlewoman of great intelligence and wit, on her journey to Egypt, where she meets Egyptologist Radcliffe Emerson (whom she ultimately marries) and foils a dastardly plot involving a mummy and assorted evil-doers, who nearly take her life. Rosenblat is the voice of so many series characters, but here too, each is distinctive, from the lilting soprano of Amelia's companion Evelyn to the hilarious rants that Amelia provokes from Emerson. Start here and listen to the entire series. You won't be disappointed.

Historical Mystery.

Other Times, Other Places: Historical Fiction

We listen to historical fiction for the same reasons we read it—to be transported back in time, to experience a culture, and to meet people from the past. These selections do that and more.

▶ **Follett, Ken**

The Pillars of the Earth. Read by John Lee. 2007. Penguin Audio. ISBN: 9780143142379. 41 hrs. ♈ ⟦Y⟧⟦A⟧ ▦

Lee whisks listeners back to 12th-century England and invites us to witness to the construction of a cathedral. Follett fills his lengthy novel with details of the process, which Lee navigates handily, turning the most mundane facts into fascinating tidbits. But this is not just about the cathedral, it's also about the people and the times, and both come alive in Lee's thoughtful rendering of character and description. Emotions and politics drive the large cast, good and bad, yet as political wrangling rages, the spires of the cathedral rise. Breathtaking to hear in all its glorious detail.

Historical Fiction.

Liss, David
The Devil's Company. **Benjamin Weaver Series.** Read by Simon Vance. 2009. Brilliance Audio. ISBN: 9781423327042. 15 hrs.

Vance's precise accents and dark tone take listeners back to 18th-century London, where thief taker Benjamin Weaver finds himself in trouble again—this time blackmailed into stealing documents from the East India Company. As he investigates why he's been set up, he uncovers a multilayered conspiracy driven by greed and betrayals. Vance is simply superb at evoking the period and characters. Through Vance's voice Weaver ponders his dilemma with genuine thoughtfulness and wit, while the secondary characters shimmer with life. Vance's smooth narration keeps us riveted to characters and story, while he also imparts Liss's wealth of historical detail.

Historical Fiction; Thriller; Literary Fiction.

See, Lisa
Snow Flower and the Secret Fan. Read by Janet Song. 2005. Books on Tape. ISBN: 1415921547. 11.25 hrs. [Y][A] 🕮

See explores the unlikely friendship of two women from disparate backgrounds and traces 19th-century Chinese cultural history and attitudes toward women in this intriguing novel. Looking back over her life, Lily, a farmer's daughter, relates the story of her friendship with Snow Flower and their method of communication through a secret language known only to women. Song embodies Lily's character in her reading, as she shares the poignant and bittersweet tale of friendship and highlights fascinating historical and cultural details.

Historical Fiction; Women's Fiction.

Stott, Rebecca
The Coral Thief. Read by Simon Prebble. 2009. Tantor Media. ISBN: 9781400113385. 9 hrs.

This elegant, atmospheric novel blends a caper with historical details and the history of science in a fascinating exploration of real and fictional characters and the scientific and philosophical thought in pre-Darwinian Europe. An English medical student on his way to study natural history in Paris in 1815 has his letters of recommendation and coral samples stolen by a beautiful woman on the coach to Paris. When he tracks her down, he becomes enamored of this philosopher thief and her approach to radical new scientific theories. Prebble's reading enhances the cast of believable characters, the edgy tone, and the gorgeous prose. This novel intriguingly combines passions, both physical and intellectual, brave new ideas, French savants, and the criminal underworld.

Historical Fiction; Literary Fiction; Caper.

Turner, Nancy E.
These Is My Words: The Diary of Sarah Agnes Prine, 1881–1901, Arizona Territories. **Sarah Agnes Prine Series.** Read by Valerie Leonard. 1999. BBC Audiobooks America/Chivers. ISBN: 9780792748816. 14.2 hrs. [Y][A] 🕮

Based on the author's great-grandmother's diary, this fascinating account reveals the mundane particulars of domestic life in Arizona Territory, where one encounters dangers and death from snakes, Indians, and more. Leonard's soft drawl draws listeners into this richly detailed story of a sensible and intelligent young woman who displays a true pioneer spirit. As she matures from a naive young girl to a remarkable wife and mother, both her grammar and writing style reflect her growth. A cast of colorful characters, touches of adventure, and authentic historical details enhance this heartwarming and heartbreaking tale.

Historical Fiction; Women's Fiction; Western.

Global Sleuthing: Mysteries around the World

Whether the focus is on police detectives, private investigators, or amateur detectives, mysteries set outside of North America and England offer intriguing glimpses into other cultures and societies, in addition to a good mystery. The following examples introduce listeners to the series, sometimes at the beginning and sometimes with an excellent example later on.

Burdett, John

Bangkok 8. **Sonchai Jitpleecheep Series.** Read by Paul Boehmer. 2003. Books on Tape. ISBN: 0736693742. 13.5 hrs.

Bangkok policeman Sonchai Jitpleecheep may be the only honest cop in town, but his life may still give listeners pause. In addition to working for the police, he helps his mother run a brothel. Murders in Bangkok's 8th Police District are particularly nasty and the villains even worse, as in this first series entry in which he investigates the bizarre murder of a U.S. Marine. Illegal markets, especially in sex and jade, and corruption on every level play roles in these gritty mysteries. Boehmer's edgy tone underlines the dangers of this menacing landscape, but he has also created interesting personas for the series characters, especially for Sonchai, whose unusual lifestyle, determined by his Buddhist philosophy, makes him a fascinating guide to an unfamiliar world. Thai words that might stop us in print roll off Boehmer's tongue, making listeners feel as if we are part of the scene. An intriguing mystery series that explores a non-Western approach to crime investigation.

Mystery; Thriller.

Kaminsky, Stuart

The People Who Walk in Darkness. **Inspector Porfiry Rostnikov Series.** Read by Daniel Oreskes. 2008. BBC Audiobooks America. ISBN: 9780792754428. 7.75 hrs.

This, the 15th title in this popular series (which began before the collapse of the Soviet Union), finds Inspector Porfiry Petrovich Rostnikov still battling crime within and without the police department. It's impossible to resist this mordant one-legged detective who visits his amputated leg (kept in formaldehyde in a laboratory) and who has survived political chaos and departmental corruption for decades. This case takes Rostnikov to Siberia to track down a diamond-smuggling ring, while his team follows other clues in Moscow and Kiev. Oreskes's lovely deep voice provides appropriate Russian accents for the dialog, while establishing the mood for this often gruesome and dark mystery. He has the tone just right: affable and sometimes almost befuddled for the persistent detective and filled with menace and sinister humor when portraying the Russian mafia villain. Listeners who wonder whether life has improved in today's Russia need only listen to this exceptional entry in this excellent series.
Mystery.

Leon, Donna
Blood from a Stone. **Guido Brunetti Series.** Read by David Colacci. 2005. Audio Partners. ISBN: 1572704683. 9.25 hrs.

Leon has a knack for combining Commisario Guido Brunetti's professional life with a thriving and fascinating family life in contemporary Venice. This entry takes us into the underground world of illegals, as Brunetti investigates the murder of a Senegalese street vendor. The sensible, compassionate Brunetti seems always caught in a web of red tape propagated by an unfeeling bureaucracy that hides political chicanery. Colacci excels at performing each of the familiar characters and pulls us into the family celebration at Christmastime, as well as into the grim investigation and the frustrations of police politics. He handles the witty dialog with ease and conveys the dry humor as well as the thoughtful consideration of important social issues. His comfortable reading captures the rhythms of Venetian life.
Mystery.

Mankell, Henning
Faceless Killers. **Kurt Wallander Series.** Read by Dick Hill. 2007. Blackstone Audiobooks. ISBN: 9780786161393. 9 hrs.

Swedish detective Kurt Wallander, faced with a brutal murder linked to foreigners, fears his investigation will lead to vicious hate crimes. The first of the series to be published in the United States, this atmospheric and grisly puzzle focuses on procedural details as well as controversial social issues. Known for his narration of many fast-paced thriller and suspense novels, Hill may seem an odd choice for this series, especially since he reads without accents. Still, his portrayal of Wallander through the first-person narration works surprisingly well, as he draws listeners into the detective's life and personal problems as well as into the action.
Mystery; Crime Thriller.

▶ **McCall Smith, Alexander**
The No. 1 Ladies' Detective Agency. **No. 1 Ladies' Detective Agency Series.**
Read by Lisette Lecat. 2003. Recorded Books. ISBN: 1402545940. 8.25 hrs.

Although the private investigator may be an American invention, they're so popular that it's no wonder that these skilled investigators have found homes elsewhere, even in somewhat exotic locales. Here, heroine Mma "Precious" Ramotswe, proprietress of a detective agency, provides a glimpse into life in Botswana through her cases that demand more of an understanding of human nature than detecting skill. Lecat, a native South African, completely captures the lilting cadence of Mma Ramotswe as well as the crew of series characters. All titles in the series offer a strong sense of place and people, and Lecat's melodious performance leaves listeners satisfied, yet hungry for more.

Mystery; Gentle Reads; Women's Fiction.

On the Road Again: Travel Narratives

Journeys have long been a popular theme in literature, both fiction and non-fiction, in film, and on audio. Whether imaginary or real, these are stories that take us there—wherever that is—and make the trip as much of a pleasure as the arrival.

▶ **Bloom, Amy**
Away. Read by Barbara Rosenblat. 2007. HighBridge. ISBN: 9781598875218. 8 hrs. ♔

Rich in unique characters and accents, Bloom's road novel stars Lillian Leyb, a Russian immigrant haunted by dreams of her family, and the myriad personalities she encounters on her journey to and across America, all effortlessly brought to life by the talented Rosenblat. When Leyb learns her daughter may have survived a massacre and could be living in Siberia, she begins the trek back again. From Russia in the 1920s to New York City and then across the United States through Alaska and back to Siberia, a story of fascinating characters and slices of history comes to life. Here is a female Ulysses who may not make it home but makes her own home in the end.

Literary Fiction; Historical Fiction.

Doctorow, E. L.
The March. Read by Joe Morton. 2005. Books on Tape. ISBN: 1415924201 11.25 hrs. ♔ ☕

Ostensibly recording General William Tecumsah Sherman's famous march to the sea in the waning months of the Civil War, Doctorow's epic tale combines a vast cast of characters, each with individual stories, with an indelibly etched landscape of the war-torn South. Morton's superb performance requires a wide range of voices and accents, which he accomplishes mostly through subtle nuance, allowing the character's language to dominate and set the tone.

Mythic in scope, this provocative novel puts listeners into the consciousness of the characters. As Morton takes us into Sherman's army, we absorb the sense of the times, sometimes dark and dangerous, sometimes bittersweet, sometimes full of ribald humor as comic relief.

Historical Fiction; Adventure; War Stories.

Heat-Moon, William Least

Blue Highways: A Journey into America. Read by Frank Muller. 2004. Recorded Books. ISBN: 9781419321504. 16 hrs. Nonfiction.

Muller's eloquent rendition enhances this classic travel memoir on the back roads of America. His effortless, evocative reading follows the ebb and flow of the journey that documents landscape, people, and impressions and explores Heat-Moon's inner journey as well as the physical one. His comfortable narration reflects Heat-Moon's curiosity and his thoughtful observations about little-known people and places. Muller's regional accents add authenticity to the journey, as this entertaining and meandering exploration of small-town America transports listeners back to a life outside of the fast lane.

Travel.

McCarthy, Cormac

The Road. Read by Tom Stechschulte. 2006. Recorded Books. ISBN: 9781428105515. 6.75 hrs. ♈ Y A ◵

Stechschulte's hypnotic reading of McCarthy's dark parable makes for a haunting, atmospheric tale, as two survivors, a father and his son, move toward hoped-for safety through a devastated postapocalyptic landscape. Stechschulte's understated performance reflects McCarthy's spare prose and adds a layer of vibrant emotion to the bleak tale, as the unnamed father is sustained by his memories and his hope in his young son. Lessons are taught and learned along the road, and life goes on in this richly evocative tale.

Literary Fiction.

Olmstead, Robert

Coal Black Horse. Read by Ed Sala. 2007. Recorded Books. ISBN: 9781428160170. 7.25 hrs. Y A

Sent by his mother to find his soldier father at Gettysburg, 14-year-old Robey Child encounters the eponymous horse, which carries him on this lyrical, but horrifying, coming-of-age journey. Sala reads with solemn tones that reflect the mood of the story—dramatic, haunting, thoughtful. Although the novel has a historical setting, details are personal and emotional, mirroring Robey's journey to manhood as he encounters the horrors of war and the dangers from both man and environment. Graceful, lyrical language, rich in images, resonates through the skilled reading.

Literary Fiction; Coming-of-Age; Historical Fiction.

Then and Now: Dual Story Lines

Many popular novels today follow story lines in both the past and present. What books do with spatial breaks and typeface, narrators must convey through pauses and differences in tone and sometimes accent. These wonderfully effective performances show us how it is done.

Brooks, Geraldine
People of the Book. Read by Edwina Wren. 2008. Blackstone. ISBN: 9781433212697. 14 hrs. 🏆 📚

As art restorer Hannah Heath works on the Sarajewo Haggadah, a priceless 15th-century sacred text, she discovers its intriguing provenance as well as the answers to questions from her own past. Artifacts within the pages take us back in time to previous owners of the book and events in the book's—and the Jewish people's—turbulent history. Wren's Australian accent matches Hannah's, but she also reflects the voices of the manuscript's owners across central Europe. Her heartfelt reading enlivens characters and events, as it mirrors Brooks's graceful prose in this thoughtful, evocative, and cinematic tale, which takes us out of our lives and into those of others.

Literary Fiction; Historical Fiction; Art.

Crook, Elizabeth
The Night Journal. Read by Kimberly Farr. 2006. Books on Tape. ISBN: 1415929289. 17.5 hrs. 🏆

Meg Mabry, great-granddaughter of a frontierswoman who settled in New Mexico, has distanced herself as much as possible from her heritage. However, when her grandmother forces her to research her past, she uncovers secrets that shake the foundation of her family history. Farr negotiates the jumps between centuries and characters with vocal shifts that leave listeners in no doubt about whether they're in Meg's contemporary world or discovering the world of her ancestor through colorful diary entries. Her thoughtful performance provides a heartwarming and nostalgic look back as well as insight into the role of the past in the present.

Historical Fiction; Western.

Fesperman, Dan
The Arms Maker of Berlin. Read by Dick Hill. 2009. Brilliance. ISBN: 9781423346661. 16 hrs.

Missing documents from wartime files send history professor Nat Turnbull to Europe and the U.S. Archives, seeking files "misplaced" by his mentor Gordon Wolfe, an historian who worked for the Office of Strategic Services (OSS) out of Switzerland during the war. The secrets contained in the missing files relate to the wartime records of Kurt Bauer, a German industrialist on whom the Allies placed their hopes of rebuilding Germany after the war, and the White Rose, a renowned group of university students who led resistance to Hitler in the early 1940s. Hill reads this compelling spy thriller with his usual deft pacing and inflection. Flashbacks to historical events and Turnbull's own investigations in the present offer similar themes: danger from unknown parties and the omnipresent question of whom to trust. A dramatic, emotionally charged, and intriguing look at the end of the Nazi era, rich in historical and spycraft details.

Thriller; Historical Fiction.

Howe, Katherine

The Physick Book of Deliverance Dane. Read by Katherine Kellgren. 2009. Books on Tape. ISBN: 9780307701978. 12.75 hrs.

Persuaded to take a break from academics to ready her grandmother's crumbling house for sale, Harvard Ph.D. candidate Connie Goodman discovers a dissertation topic as well as a family secret when she comes across a scrap of paper referring to Deliverance Dane. Who was she, and why is there no trace of her in Colonial records? And what is the connection between the woman and the strange powers Connie seems to possess? While the contemporary story line dominates, Howe also offers the historical details that explore the creation of Dane's book and its provenance, including the fate of its author. Kellgren's exceptional performance leads listeners on a fascinating journey through modern academics and Colonial history, including the Salem witch trials. The supernatural seems real in Kellgren's hands, and her vocal skill animates this emotionally charged tale, filled with intriguing characters.

Literary Fiction; Historical Fiction.

▶ Turow, Scott

Ordinary Heroes. Read by Edward Herrmann. 2005. Books on Tape. ISBN: 9781415924822. 13.75 hrs.

With story lines past and present and tales of both father and son, Turow's thoughtful novel follows retired newspaperman Stewart Dubinsky as he discovers letters and a memoir that chronicle his father's wartime experience—and uncovers a family secret. Herrmann's masterful, unhurried narration and his facility with accents and voices take listeners to a variety of times and places. However, his voice more dramatically reflects the emotional layer of these stories and their impact, as well as Turow's elegant prose. Herrmann moves smoothly from the edgy intensity of battle scenes and wartime skulduggery to the thoughtful ruminations of a son exploring his father's unexpected history. An evocative, investigative tale of the nature of truth and the stories that become our past.

Historical Fiction; War Stories.

Starring Mother Nature: Weather-Based Stories

Whether you prefer your days sunny and bright or overcast and gloomy, you'll find weather playing a crucial role in many books, fiction and nonfiction. Pick your favorite weather disaster and match it to a good tale!

Brown, Sandra
Chill Factor. Read by Stephen Lang. 2005. Recorded Books. ISBN: 1419375482. 13.5 hrs.

A blizzard in the North Carolina mountains traps Lilly Martin, ex-wife of a police chief, in a cabin with writer Ben Tierney, stranded when his car broke down. Is he the good guy he seems—or the serial murderer sought by police? Lang sets the stage for suspense early on, and our discomfort builds in this claustrophobic environment where every action seems suspicious. The shiver we feel isn't just the result of the cold!

Suspense; Weather.

▶ **Burke, James Lee**
The Tin Roof Blowdown. **Dave Robicheaux Series.** Read by Will Patton. 2007. Recorded Books. ISBN: 9781428155855. 13 hrs. ☃

Many books, fiction and nonfiction, have explored 2005's Hurricane Katrina and the devastation of New Orleans, but few have done so with the power and compelling vision of this mystery, the 16th in Burke's Dave Robicheaux series. While the storm provides its center, this is also a complex, layered mystery, and Patton voices the gruff, seen-it-all Detective Robicheaux to perfection. In contrast, his portrayal of the psychopath villain chills with a matter-of-fact blandness. Narrator Patton's heartfelt performance of this dark journey of the soul underscores Burke's lyrical prose as he takes us through the nightmare of the storm and its aftermath.

Mystery; Literary Fiction; Weather.

Kallos, Stephanie
Sing Them Home. Read by Tavia Gilbert. 2009. Blackstone Audiobooks. ISBN: 9781433203367. 19.5 hrs.

Blame it on the weather—a tornado, in fact, which carries Hope Jones away from a small Nebraska town in 1978 and initiates this saga of a family destroyed and made whole again. Gilbert's hypnotic narration reveals the essence of every character and even makes the dead, who comment on events, a kind of Greek chorus never far removed from the action. After all, death and weather are the most certain and uncertain elements in life. Lyrical prose, leavened by whimsical wit, detailed character-centered stories revealed in flashbacks, and Gilbert's splendid rendition of Welsh songs, make this a somewhat sentimental but immensely satisfying tale.

Literary Fiction; Weather.

Larson, Erik

Isaac's Storm: A Man, a Time, and the Deadliest Hurricane in History. Read by Richard M. Davidson. 2000. Recorded Books. ISBN: 9781428109681. 9 hrs. Nonfiction.

Larson turns to the diaries of Galveston's chief meteorologist Isaac Cline, as well as to other firsthand sources, to report this fascinating true tale of the monstrous hurricane that devastated Galveston, Texas, in September, 1900, leaving an estimated 8,000 dead. Cline considered himself a scientist who could predict the weather, but missed reports and ignored warnings proved again how difficult that is to do. Davidson's well-paced reading builds the tension, and makes the meticulous detail enthralling. We may know what will happen, but his serious tone heightens the sense of menace and emotional intensity.

Weather.

Pickard, Nancy

The Virgin of Small Plains. Read by Kymberly Dakin. 2006. BBC Audiobooks America. ISBN: 0792740572. 11.25 hrs. ♛

Pickard invokes a strong sense of place in her depiction of the Kansas Flint Hills, which have seasonal storms that reflect the changeable Kansas weather and underline the novel's dangerous tone. Both the vividly described winter blizzard and summer tornado ring true to any listener who has experienced nature's wrath. The dramatic weather builds a irresistible sense of foreboding, as former lovers Abby Reynolds and Mitch Newquist meet again as adults and feel compelled to investigate the murder of a classmate and the subsequent cover-up that separated them years earlier. Dakin's reading reveals an intriguing group of small-town characters and their emotions and motivations, as the truth of the crime is finally discovered.

Mystery; Weather.

Wide-Open Spaces:
Stories Set in the Great Outdoors

For those times when we want to escape, to travel away from the bustle of cities and towns, we can explore new territory in these books set in the great outdoors.

Barr, Nevada

Flashback. **Anna Pigeon Series.** Read by Barbara Rosenblat. 2003. Recorded Books. ISBN: 140254197X. 16 hrs.

The books in this series are the perfect accompaniment on a trip to one of the national parks. Barr's ranger Anna Pigeon has been posted in parks around the United States, and in each she explores flora, fauna, and landscape—and solves a good mystery. If you're not traveling, pick the park you've always wanted to visit, and relax in your armchair as Anna faces murderous land-scapes and villains. Rosenblat, who has narrated the entire series for Recorded Books, captures both the strength and vulnerability of our heroine in these intimate character portraits. Be advised, however, that these tales also reflect the deadliness of the natural landscape. *Flashback*, set in the Dry Tortugas, has mysteries past and present, set at the old fort and involving one of Anna's ancestors and her letters.

Mystery; Historical Fiction.

Braun, Matt

Dakota. Read by Jack Garrett. 2006. Recorded Books. ISBN: 9781419381867. 12.5 hrs. ♈

After the deaths of his wife and his mother, Teddy Roosevelt escapes to Dakota Territory to restore his spirit in this Spur Award–winning inspirational biographical tale, which also explores frontier history. Garrett ably contrasts Roosevelt's educated cadences with those of the settlers and ranchers, and his engaging drawl captures the thoughtful, heartwarming tone of the novel, as well as the homespun humor. In this environment, which promotes both con-templation and action (Teddy kills a grizzly), listeners will recognize both the danger and beauty of the landscape and its power to heal.

Historical Fiction; Western; Biographical Novels.

Enger, Leif

Peace Like a River. Read by Chad Lowe. 2008. Harper Audio. ISBN: 9780061457876. 11.5 hrs. ♈ [Y][A] 🐦

In Enger's powerful story of love and family, a young man commits a crime to protect his family and then escapes from jail, traveling west from Minnesota in the 1960s to the Badlands and beyond. Multiple story lines and vividly drawn characters intertwine perfectly as the complex tale unfolds, re-vealing a provocative story of miracles, journey, adventure, and family. Lowe's fresh, young voice captures the 11-year-old narrator's spirit and naiveté with its confiding, intimate tone. He reads without accent and without assigning distinctive voices to each character and thus allows the gorgeous prose and rich images to enthrall listeners. As in Westerns, it is the landscape of the wide-open spaces that offers redemption.

Literary Fiction; Mystery.

▶ Hillerman, Tony

The Shape Shifter. **Joe Leaphorn and Jim Chee Series.** Read by George Guidall. 2006. Recorded Books. ISBN: 9781419390074. 7 hrs. ♈ [Y][A]

Hillerman's layered mysteries evoke the Four Corners region of the Ameri-can Southwest with detailed landscapes and a sometimes mystical view of the area and its people. In this late entry in the series, retired Navajo policeman Lt. Joe Leaphorn is drawn back into a cold case involving a murderer and a cursed Navajo rug. His former assistant Jim Chee helps solve the dangerous case, once again focused on Navajo customs and artifacts. Series narrator Guidall's smooth, nuanced reading brings the world of the reservation to life. With his silky voice, he inhabits the series characters and creates a tangible landscape—vast miles of open spaces for villains to hide in and the relentless police to investigate.

Mystery; Western.

Krueger, William Kent
Copper River. **Cork O'Connor Series.** Read by David Chandler. 2006. Recorded Books. ISBN: 9781428122826. 10 hrs.

Krueger is known for his vivid descriptions of the wild and dangerous beauty of the upper Midwest. Here, his hero policeman Cork O'Connor is back in the Upper Peninsula of Michigan, chased by a hired killer and hiding out in a cousin's cabin. Chandler's tone contrasts the cinematic beauty of the rugged landscape with the vulnerability of one man on the run. He sets the scene for the varied cast members, each easily distinguished, including both men and women as well as a smart-mouthed teenager. Plot twists and deadly danger abound; listeners will revel in the lyrical prose interspersed with grisly images in this series mystery.

Mystery; Thriller.

The Wild West, Then and Now

The West remains a mythical landscape—a place where one can get a new start and make one's way, a place of unexplored treasures, a place to which one can escape the crowds of the industrialized East. But times change and so do the stories—or some of them. Themes from standard Westerns continue to resonate in these tales of the modern West.

Box, C. J.
Blue Heaven. Read by John Bedford Lloyd. 2008. BBC Audiobooks America. ISBN: 9780792752295. 12 hrs. ♟

Told in a spare dialog that recalls the language of classic Westerns, this novel of the modern West features good guys and bad, but this time the bad guys are retired cops. Lloyd's deep voice perfectly captures the grave tone and the character of the rancher/hero, while lighter tones reflect the two young children who, having witnessed the cops murder a man in the woods, are on the run, not knowing whom to trust. Lloyd keeps listeners on the edge of their chairs with this haunting, evocative, emotional tale of the dangers abroad in the new West.

Suspense; Western.

Johnson, Craig
Death without Company. **Walt Longmire Series.** Read by George Guidall. 2007. Recorded Books. ISBN: 9781428129337. 10 hrs.

Johnson's popular Walt Longmire mystery series, set in Wyoming, evokes the feel of the West—old and new. The cadenced and colorful language lends itself to audio, with the lush descriptions of the stark landscape and the intriguing, fully rounded characters. The cast is a cultural mix of longtime residents, including Indians and Basques, and Longmire's quirky staff. Guidall's gruff, laconic voice accurately reflects the aging widower police chief, who refuses to give up on a lead. A compelling blend of dark secrets, action, and interesting series characters.

Western; Mystery.

L'Amour, Louis

High Lonesome. Read by David Strathairn. 2008. Books on Tape. ISBN: 9781415947111. 3.5 hrs.

Few authors have found such a splendid interpreter of their works as David Strathairn is for L'Amour's classic tales of the Old West. With luck, he'll record them all, imbuing them with new life and attracting a new audience to these old-fashioned morality tales. His slight twang and reserved reading take listeners back to another time and place. In this non-series title, Considine and his crew rob a purportedly impregnable bank to take revenge, but while escaping, they encounter a young woman and her father, pursued by Apaches. Escape or help? L'Amour's heroes, tight-lipped but noble, always choose the hard way. Strathairn transports readers back in time in this elegiac story that blends action, adventure, and, perhaps surprisingly, reflection.

Western.

McGarrity, Michael

Death Song. **Kevin Kerney Series.** Read by George Guidall. 2008. Recorded Books. ISBN: 9781428164185. 8.5 hrs.

The impact of Westerns derives as much from the quintessential battle between good and evil as it does from the mythical landscape, and Guidall's expressive rendition of McGarrity's gorgeous descriptions of the harsh environment will take readers back to the 19th century. The bad guys—in this case drug traffickers—may be more modern, but the setting, often traversed on horseback, evokes earlier days. Police chief Kevin Kerney tackles one more case before his retirement, and frequent series-narrator Guidall steps right into the character, exposing psychological ruminations as well as a dry wit. Engaging characters, a twisting plot, and evocative landscapes come alive in Guidall's comfortable performance.

Mystery; Western.

Parker, Robert B.

Appaloosa. **Virgil Cole and Everett Hitch Series.** Read by Titus Welliver. 2005. Books on Tape. ISBN: 1415921369. 5 hrs.

Although better known for his Boston-set P.I. mysteries, Parker also made successful excursions into the Western genre, as in the first in a series featuring lawmen Virgil Cole and Everett Hitch. Roaming through the West, they clean up towns like Appaloosa. Welliver's deep voice resonates with the cadences of the Old West, capturing the colorful language, the dark tone, the cinematic landscape, and the moral dilemmas faced by men who live by a code of honor. For fans of Westerns as well as tales of male friendship.

Western; Historical Fiction.

Index

133

About the Author

Although JOYCE G. SARICKS has retired from the readers' advisory desk at the Downers Grove Public Library, she continues to speak, write, and provide workshops on readers' advisory and to teach at Dominican University's (Illinois) Graduate School of Library and Information Science. She is the author of *Readers' Advisory Service in the Public Library* and *The Readers' Advisory Guide to Genre Fiction*. In addition to writing for EBSCO's NoveList, she reviews audiobooks and writes a monthly column on readers' advisory for *Booklist*.